JAKE IVIE

# CHOCOLATE MOOSE
## A MILITARY FAMILY'S DOG WHO TRAVELED THE WORLD"

*Moose as a puppy with sawdust on his head and Jake*

# TABLE OF CONTENTS

Chapter 1: Adoption a New Beginning                    1

Chapter 2: Part of a Growing Family                    15

Chapter 3: The European Adventure                     44

Chapter 4: Adventures in Japan                        78

Chapter 5: The Journey Home                           90

Chapter 6: The Big Scare and Decline in Health       109

Chapter 7: Saying Goodbye                            122

Chapter 8: Learning to Move On                       138

About the Author                                     152

# PROLOGUE

This work is a product birthed from the need for me to find a method to cope with the loss of my Chocolate Lab after fourteen and a half years of his loyalty to our family. It tells the story of how a dog touched the lives of people across three continents. It tells the story of extreme highs and lows, of tragedies and miracles. It recalls how the love from a dog named Moose change me and my family and taught us about love and sacrifice. My hope is that the story will make you laugh and maybe make you cry, but above all I hope you as the reader will glean some bit of inspiration. Lastly, maybe just maybe this story will help someone who is suffering through the loss of a beloved pet. I dedicate this book to all the puppy parents who have suffered the loss of a fur baby and for those who always treat their dogs as part of the family. I would also like to thank my wife, Odie, for her patience and recollection of key details to make this book complete.

# Chapter 1:
# Adoption: A New Beginning

It was a horrible feeling knowing that this final trip to the vet would be Moose's last "appointment." The mood was grim but deliberate. He had lived for fourteen and a half years with us through five moves across three continents. My big boy had been to more places in that amount of time than most people and the precious memories stacked up. He had taught us to love, and the pain we were feeling could only be matched by the joy he brought to us for a decade and a half. His final moments would end in a suburban house in Oklahoma where they started. This is the story of a dog who touched the lives of every member of our family and extended into the lives of countless people who had the pleasure of meeting Moose. It's the story of a Chocolate lab whose compassion and love for life are worth telling. This is the story of Moose.

*The online advertisement that made us fall in love.*

I don't remember exactly where or how the conversation with my wife, Odie, started about adopting a new puppy, but I do remember we settled on the Labrador. It could have been because of the crazy mix of a Lab and Husky personified in Ginger, whom Odie reluctantly agreed to adopt after the kids begged her before we even started dating. She became the fourth kid in our ready-made mixed family after we got married. I became the stepdad to three humans, a cat named Sammie, who passed while we lived in Florida, and a dog. After we settled on a Labrador, I began the research in the spring of 2009. I looked online for the best breeders in Oklahoma City. I found a few websites that bragged about the lineage and their reputations for show dogs, but they seemed obtuse and out of touch with what we were looking for. My perception was that these breeders were out to make a buck by selling pedigree pups to the highest bidder, who lived in a home far more extravagant than we could afford as a military family. So, the search went on.

As a native Okie returning home from five assignments over ten years away from home, I wanted a lab that was more indicative of my roots. Odie would argue that I was not a country boy at all, but the roots of my upbringing drew me to a simpler kind of "good boy." I started looking for hunting dogs who were bred to retrieve birds in the way retrievers are trained. Knowing my wife was right, as all husbands understand at some point (usually too late), I pursued my quest for the perfect breeder.

I'll break here to discuss the controversy between breeders, puppy farms, and adoption facilities. In my humble opinion, it doesn't matter. As long as a dog is loved and included as part of the family, he or she will always be part of the family. Now that I am older, fourteen and a half years after we adopted Moose, we have a German Shepherd from a breeder in Italy, a stray tiger-striped mixed cat from OKC, and five grand fur babies from the kids. Those constitute an "Oki" mix from Okinawa, an adopted lab and pit mix from Oklahoma City, a lab and Weimaraner mix, a full-bred Husky, and another German Shepherd from our in-laws. There are those who preach about the evils of seeking a purebred and the disasters of adoptions from a shelter. In my experience, one is not worse or better. It all boils down to the love you give because it is received tenfold from an animal. Animals are... quite frankly... better at loving than humans. I once heard it said that the reason our furry companions don't live as long as us is that it doesn't take them as long to learn how to love.

It was that love that we as a family were about to experience when I finally found a website for a breeder in eastern Oklahoma called Perry's Pups. The website is no longer active, but they were advertising four pups at the time. Two chocolates, a yellow and a black. When we saw the one that melted our hearts, we immediately began the coordination. This was in May of 2009, just after we closed on our house. His picture showed him in a basket wearing a black collar. We were in love. I contacted the people and mailed them a check. The bill of sale was hand-written and included the names of his parents, Rocky and Starr. In the space for a name, it simply said "Black," the color of his collar. Thus began the debate of what we were to name him. I don't remember what the alternative options were, but we settled on Moose as a play of words - chocolate mousse. Little did we know how prophetic that name would be until we soon learned how sweet of a demeanor he would have.

He still wasn't weened, so we wouldn't be able to pick him up until later in May. We had already planned a Memorial Day trip from Oklahoma City to Missouri to see my parents Randall and Debbie in a tiny town between Springfield and Branson called Spokane. They live out in the country, so we took Ginger with us. The weekend was filled with conversations about how we would stop by Wyandotte, Oklahoma, to meet and bring home our newest member of the family, a companion for Ginger. It was this weekend when Ginger escaped and, being the Husky mix she was, ran like the wind across the Ozark hills, a trend that will play a major role in a story yet to be told. Luckily, fate determined she would be retrieved. We finished our visit with my parents and my sisters Tiffany and Joanna and set off again for Oklahoma with the buzzing of anticipation for the first time we would meet Moose.

We left Spokane and set off on hilly roads in our nine-passenger SUV towards the small town, where we would encounter a small, manufactured home with a barn on the property about 100 feet from the house. We had texted ahead with our estimated arrival time, and the caretakers of our little friend were waiting on the front porch. They coincidentally also bred pugs, so when we showed up, I saw a pug puppy scampering about. I initially thought this to be our long-awaited fur baby, but my preconceived notion of the size of a lab puppy tainted my judgment. Nope, Moose came around the corner and was twice the size of the pug. He was scampering about with his soft lab ears (the softest thing on the planet) flapping away. When we got out of the car, he immediately came to investigate his new family. His little tail was wagging furiously as we picked him up. The sheer joy of picking up your new puppy for the first time is unmatched. The kids were doting on him and playing with him as I completed the transaction of the best $450 I ever spent. We signed some paperwork, told the nice people 'thank you,' and situated our new member of the family in the back seat between Chelsey and Kyle on his brand-new puppy bed.

I'll never forget his cute little face sitting on that seat as he laid down all comfy. I can only imagine his confusion as this was the first of many road trips he would experience. I remember smelling poop, and after a short investigation saw he had been stepping in it. He also had a front paw that was rubbed raw, probably from being in the barn on the hard concrete. We cleaned him up and determined he would never sleep outdoors again since our family was ready to spoil him rotten.

As I drove, I was insanely jealous that I couldn't be in the back seat with Moose. I did manage to capture glimpses of him from time to time and was overwhelmed by his cuteness. Ginger was in the back of her kennel, but she could tell something was up. The trip home was uneventful. We pulled into the driveway and started showing Moose around his new house. Ginger was indifferent. He would go up and sniff her, but she didn't seem to want to have much to do with him. We fed him for the first time and learned that he *loved* eating, which is very typical of Labradors.

Being new puppy parents was challenging. We knew we were supposed to potty train him and teach him tricks but had no idea how to do all that. Ginger came by it naturally since she was an outside dog for a long time. We were flying by the seat of our pants with Moose. Luckily, we'd soon find out how easy he would be to train. Our house had carpet in the living room and tile in the kitchen, so we decided to put two baby gates up to keep him corralled in the kitchen for the night. We put a puppy pad on the floor and made sure he had water in his bowl. We admired him as we told him good night and that we loved him. Then we sent the kids to bed, and Odie and I retired to the master bedroom. It had been a long day, so I fell asleep as soon as my head hit the pillow.

I don't remember how long I had been asleep, but I was awoken by a blood-curdling howl that sounded like someone was torturing a baby human. I sprung out of bed startled and soon realized that Moose was the source of the noise that had caused my heart to leap out of my chest. I opened the door and walked into the kitchen. The poor little guy was terrified and suffering from being displaced from his litter mates. When he saw me, he wagged his tail and looked up at me. Don't judge me, but I just couldn't help myself. I picked him up and took him outside to use the bathroom. I was so groggy. I don't remember if he went, but I do remember that we decided to bring him into the room with us and kennel-train him. He never once slept in another room again. We were attached for life.

We kenneled him for a short while, but it wasn't long before he was sleeping through the night and not making messes. He would start whining if he needed to go out, which made it easy to potty train him. He had a few messes here and there, but they were rare, and soon it became a routine. Once he was able to make it through the night, we started letting him sleep on the bed. It was the first time I had ever let a dog sleep in our bed. Ginger would sleep with the kids, but our room was off-limits. I guess those big yellow eyes and those soft, floppy ears have a way of changing people. The companionship was solidified between my dog, Moose, and me. Soon, he would learn to meet other people.

That moment came when Odie had to leave to take the kids somewhere. At the time, I was in formal military training with no option to take leave, so I was left to fend for myself... and three other fur nerds. By this time, we had an orange Tabby cat named Ike, a Husky-Lab mix, Ginger, and a Labrador puppy. No one would let Moose out during the day while I was in training. I was at an impasse. We were forced to return to containing our pup in the kitchen through baby gates. We knew there would be much collateral damage, but we had no choice. I was doing solo-parent operations; I had to own it and figure out a way forward.

Like any military guy, I called in for reinforcements. My buddy Tony was in class with me, and he just so happened to be a temp bachelor for the week since his wife and two adorable kids had also abandoned him on a temporary road trip. As all dudes do, we agreed every day would be a sleepover, and we would ride to work together. He unwillingly became a second parent to Moose, which proved to be a heavy lift since we had to leave him alone all day long, penned up in the kitchen.

Every day, we would leave, do our thing at work as Air Battle Manager students, and return to the house. The transit time to and from was about thirty minutes. Adding an extra hour, my poor little buddy was left alone. He had Ginger there with him, but it hurt me knowing he was isolated from her in the kitchen all day.

Tony and I established a routine when we would get home. Normally, the first thing I do is take off my flight suit uniform, or my monkey suit as I call it, but Moose was always a mess. The first step was getting him cleaned up. Tony was assigned this task even though I preferred it over my chore. After picking him up and greeting him with his little tail wagging, I would hand him over to Tony, who would take him out back and hose off the urine and poop from his paws. My task was to clean the floor. It was cumbersome at first, but I developed a technique of cleaning the floor and putting peroxide on the grout to kill the ammonia smell from the urine. This was the only time he chewed anything. The victim was the MDF trim under the cabinets. After he was all cleaned up, Tony and I would change out of our uniforms and head upstairs to watch TV. Moose was always right behind us.

When Saturday rolled around, Tony stayed at the house since neither of our better halves had returned. Moose had an appointment that day to get his booster shots. The three of us piled into the truck and headed to the vet. Imagine two married heterosexual men walking into a vet with a chocolate lab puppy. This was Oklahoma in 2009, so you can imagine the funny looks we received. Other than being mistaken for a gay couple, the only notable event was when Moose howled like a banshee when they took his temperature from his little rump. That was the last time he howled like that, but it broke my heart. Every other time at the vet seemed to be a pleasurable experience for him since he was always a social butterfly in any setting. We were beginning to see the characteristics that would define his personality and how his little quirks would create memories for a lifetime.

Tony had this to say about Moose when I reached out to him: "Moose was such a great dog! He was a handsome boy. I remember coming over to your place in Oklahoma while we were going through training and Moose was like a bull in a china shop while still getting used to his growing body. His tail had a mind of its own and I remember him whacking it against the island area and walls because he was excited. He loved being around people and his memory lives on in all of us and this book!"

Moose and Ginger got along great, but Ginger was a runner, which caused us to be constantly on guard. She would get out, and it was always a huge ordeal. I was bound and determined that I would train Moose to come when called. My grandmother, Mommom, as all of us grandkids called her, told me not to use whistling because many people train their dogs to come when they whistle, which presented a danger of kidnapping. She recommended clapping hands three times and then reinforcing the behavior. So, the training began.

Training him to come when called wasn't hard because he followed us everywhere. Odie and I joked that he should have been named "Shadow" because he was always underfoot. We were his pack, and he didn't want to leave us. I started in a safe environment in the backyard and clapped three times, calling, "Moose, come here, boy!" He would return and get praise. I also kept puppy food in my pocket and would feed him a piece after giving him lots of pets. It was summertime, so I frequently worked in the garage, enjoying the warm weather. I would take him with me and even give him his own screwdriver, which I still have in my toolbox as a reminder of him.

The garage was the true test. I was deathly afraid he would start running and get hit by a passing car. Luckily, our neighborhood was quiet and presented no immediate danger. I would do my woodworking, and he never got scared when I would turn on the noisy table saw. As a matter of fact, he would lay at my feet as I was working. After I made one of the cuts to build his personalized toy box, I looked down, and he was covered in sawdust, looking up at me with a confused expression. Of course, I took him inside to show Mom, who took this moment as a photo opportunity.

*Moose the carpenter*

After returning to the garage, I watched the tiny furball out of the corner of my eye as his courage and curiosity compelled him to start wandering. I started by clapping and calling as he started to leave the garage. He returned every time, receiving the same reward: pets and treats. I began to think to myself, "There is no way it is this easy!" Eventually, I would let him leave the garage and get just out of sight. I would wait about ten seconds and then call him. He returned. I waited fifteen seconds. He came back. Twenty seconds, He always came back.

We would continue this routine every weekend until he ventured too close to the street one day. I knew I had to adjust my training techniques. I needed a way of alerting him to danger. My first instinct was a deep and loud, "Moose!" That little fart stopped dead in his tracks. His tail stopped wagging, and he looked back at me with an alarmed expression as if to say, "What did I do, Dad?" It worked! Holy moly! It worked! I paused momentarily in awe that he stopped and then clapped three times and cheerfully said, "Good boy! Come here, buddy!" He got extra treats that time.

Soon, he was going with me everywhere. Mowing the yard, edging, taking out the trash, and sweeping the porch. These were all activities I always despised, but having him there made them not only tolerable but also enjoyable. He would go with me on a beer run or to the hardware store and ride in the front seat with his head barely sticking out over the window. The looks we got were great. Passengers in nearby cars would tap one another and point. Some would wave, and some would lip the words, "AWWW! How cute!" He was a handsome boy, and he had a way with the ladies too. Women of all ages would dote over him. I thought to myself, "All a guy needs is a dog. Wish I'd have known that in my younger years!"

I was careful with taking him places in the summer and would often leave the truck running but locked. This was before the day when stores would let dogs in, so he wasn't allowed in most places. I would come out of the store and see him in the driver's seat. It was like a cartoon where dogs are people and doing people things. I soon began to realize he was more lovable than most people if not all people. I adopted the philosophy that if the zombie apocalypse ever happened, I would feed Moose before people. When I would vocalize this, it was usually met with a chuckle followed by "No. Really. I'm not joking." The looks on some people's faces.

The philosophy was valid! He was part of my family and my loyal companion. He would die for me, and that is a rare bond that few people experience. My favorite part of my day would be coming home from work. I could hear him barking and looking out the window. His bark wasn't like a normal dog's, though. It was more of a deep braying like a bloodhound when he picked up a trail or a black and tan raccoon dog when she trees a possum. It wasn't an angry bark, rather, more of a, "Hey everybody! Dad's home! Come look!" I would then walk in and be greeted by the happiest soul. It didn't matter how bad or good my day was... how tired or frustrated I was. Moose was happy to see me. There was no better feeling.

The early years were great with Moose. We started to learn his behavior patterns, likes and wants, and dislikes. Our hearts grew as fast and as big as he did. Before long, he was an 80-pound dead weight on the bed – competing for covers, but with a warmth that permeated the physical senses as well as the psychological. He was a bonafide part of the family and was here to stay. Even though his appearance was like every other Chocolate Lab I've ever seen, his personality was unique.

# CHAPTER 2:

# PART OF A GROWING FAMILY

F amily. What does that really mean? People throw the word around all the time. In the military, we talk about being a family. Close friends are sometimes considered family. But what do we really mean by family? The word comes from the Latin *familia,* which means "household." Webster defines it as "the basic unit in society traditionally consisting of two parents rearing their children." I would argue that family are those souls with whom you share enough experiences to develop a bond based on trust. It's not limited to blood relatives. I'm a stepparent, and I would die for my family. I also don't think it is limited to species. How many times do you see two animals in nature bonding under the umbrella of friendship? No, I would say the idea of family extends beyond the conventional idea of a father, a mother, and children. It includes any living being that needs love and can reciprocate love. If I wrote the dictionary, I would put Moose's picture under the definition of family because that's what he was.

I struggled with the organization of this chapter for this reason: although Moose's life was chronological, the memories overlap with one another. There are so many characteristics to his personality that tie into one another in a way that makes a chronological account insufficient. So bear with me as I attempt to explain the depth of Moose's character and how his personality shaped not only my outlook on life but so many others.

*Photo opportunity with (left to right) Ginger, Brittany, Kyle, and Chelsey*

Moose was an adorable puppy, but as he grew, he wasn't any less adorable. Puppies are great, but Moose always had a puppy mentality. They say a dog never gets past the cognitive skills of a three-year-old human, so maybe that explains why Moose never grew old from a personality perspective. I have, however, seen other dogs get old and grumpy. I think a better explanation is that Moose was just a special case.

The very first personality trait we noticed in Moose was his playfulness. Being a retriever, he loved to play fetch. When he was still a puppy, the tennis balls could barely fit in his mouth, but he somehow managed to chase them and bring them back after they were thrown. The first few times we played with him were hilarious because he didn't have the coordination to stop. I would throw the ball, and he would take off in a sprint after it. Once he neared the ball, he would dip his head to pick it up with the rest of his chubby little body, carrying the momentum from a full sprint. He would tumble head over heels in the grass, pick himself up, and trot back triumphantly with the ball.

Another hilarious memory was how he would play with the soccer ball. He figured out a way to hook his tiny teeth in the seams and carry the ball that was more than twice the size of his head. He would trot sideways because the giant ball would obstruct his view, then he would bring it back for the next kick. He became very agile, and the soccer turned into a game of whether I could get it past him. I'd attempt to kick it over his head, and he would leap and block it. I'll admit that a few times, my competitive spirit sparked some overly aggressive kicks. Moose took a couple of face-shots, but he always took it like a champ and got right back into playtime.

As Moose grew older, he continued to love the standard game of fetch, but we started training him to up his game. We started teaching him to catch the tennis ball in the house. I would lightly toss it in the air, and he would catch it in his mouth. We had the sectional couch in the center of the living room, and he would run around it, making a victory lap every time he would catch the ball. Playtime also became a staple for kids who would come to the house. Moose would play with them to exhaustion. On one occasion, I was distracted by hosting a large crowd and completely forgot about Moose being outside with the kids. It was over 90 degrees outside, and he just wouldn't stop. Luckily, I intervened in time and brought him inside. He turned out to be alright, but I was worried when he laid down on the tile floor, rapidly panting with his tongue hanging out for about 15 minutes before his breathing returned to normal.

*An early love for tennis balls*

Another common Labrador trait that Moose personified was his love for water. When he was about four months old, we made a summer trip to my hometown of Ponca City about an hour and a half away from Oklahoma City. We packed up the kids and the dogs as I hitched up my 18-foot aluminum hull bass boat and hit the road. On this occasion, my aunt had some friends who owned a dock on Lake Ponca.

We drove out to the lake, taking Moose with us. We left Ginger at Mommom's house since we didn't want to have to worry about her running off, but Moose had proven to be trustworthy. My cousins were the same age as my kids, so they all came. We unloaded the car and started toward the dock.

Moose was off-leash, loving all the people around. As we approached the dock, he galloped down some stone steps toward the water. Odie didn't grow up around water and has a slight fear of lakes and rivers. I'd seen plenty of lakes, ponds, and rivers and knew that dogs had an inherent instinct of knowing how to swim. As I watched Moose, I knew what was about to happen and felt comfortable with my proximity to get to him in time. Odie was not as confident as I was, so when Moose got to the shoreline and dove straight into the water about two feet deep, Odie freaked out as Moose's head went underwater; he was under for about three seconds before I went over and picked him up by the scruff of his neck. He was probably up to about 25 pounds at the time, but being soaking wet made him a little heavier. His eyes were wide open, and he was looking at me in shock over what had just happened. I picked him up and put him on the dock to shake off the water. He had learned a valuable lesson.

The rest of the day was great. There were plenty of photo opportunities as Moose would jokingly be fitted with a life preserver and swim with the kids. Our daughter Chelsey kept very close tabs on him and made sure that if he was struggling, she was able

*The dock by Lake Ponca in Oklahoma*

to grab him. He got a chance to take a boat ride as I hooked up the tube and took my cousins out on the lake to go tubing. Aside from Moose getting unexpectedly baptized, the only other highlight was when I got pulled over for not following the correct procedures when pulling a tube. We were the only skiers on the lake, so I just nodded and apologized. What made me proud of Moose that day was his courage. Many dogs would have been traumatized by nearly drowning, but he wasn't scared at all. It was a testament to his resiliency, bravery, and toughness.

As summer ended, fall approached, and soon it was winter. Moose was almost a year old when he had his

*Swimming with Chelsey in Lake Ponca.*

first encounter with snow. Oklahoma is not known for getting the good wet snow that sticks and makes great snowmen. No, Oklahoma winters usually have dry snow, lots of cold wind, and the occasional ice storm. We got lucky during Moose's first winter, however. A storm came in and dropped about a foot of snow overnight. Since Oklahoma hardly ever gets snow, no one knows how to drive with poor road conditions, and the city doesn't invest in the same equipment that some of the northern cities have. All this to say, I wasn't going to work that day, and the kids' school was canceled. The backyard was a playground for Ginger and Moose.

Ginger had never really liked to play fetch or tug of war. She was part Husky, and she loved to run. We adopted her in Tucson, so she rarely saw snow, but when we let her and Moose out, it was like someone had set her tail on fire. Moose reacted the same way. They were jumping through the snow and shoving their faces in it. Moose and Ginger had finally found something that they could both enjoy. They stayed out there for quite a while, putting little puppy prints in the snow. Unfortunately, it was short-lived because the sun came out the next day and melted the snow away. I will always cherish the memory of how well they played together in that one foot of snow in our backyard.

Another common ground that Moose and Ginger shared was their love for rawhide bones. Ginger would bully Moose even when we would buy two of them. I would have to act as the enforcer when Ginger stole his bone and sat on hers. He would just sit there watching her chew his bone with a disappointed look on his face. It was innocent and cute but heartbreaking at the same time because I could easily draw parallels between what he was experiencing and what some children experienced. I never let it go on too far and would usually bring Moose upstairs so he could enjoy his bone in peace away from his big sister. He was more spoiled than she was, but I don't feel guilty about it. Moose was the baby of the family – that's how it works.

This dog was so spoiled that he had his own toy box with his name on it, which I mentioned building in the first chapter. It was filled with toys we would buy for him whenever we went to the pet store. Many dogs love to destroy their toys and find the squeaker or rip out the stuffing or both. Moose didn't tear up his toys. He had a few favorite ones, but his all-time favorite one was his duck. We would tell him, "Find your duck!" and he would dig in the toy box until he found the little toy. Then he would bring it to us. Bringing toys was also a common behavior when we would have guests. He would sniff them and get some initial pets, then he would retrieve a toy and bring it to them, almost as an offering of good faith to our guests. He was a gentle and kind soul who made friends everywhere he went.

We had an orange tabby cat named Ike who passed very unexpectedly while we were on vacation for Christmas. Moose got along with him okay, but it wasn't like they were best buds. A few months after Ike passed, Odie and I were headed to the local watering hole for some drinks and relaxation. On the way, she turned to me and said, "I want a kitty." I thought to myself, "Well, I guess we aren't going to the bar!" We went to a shelter to check out the kittens. I had my eye on a little smokey gray dude who was obviously rambunctious, but he didn't really resonate with what Odie was wanting. Then she spotted a tiny little female kitten with a broken tail, presumably from getting caught in a cage door. She was obviously the runt, but Odie has a thing for underdogs, so we drew up the paperwork and took her home.

She and Moose hit it off great! We have pictures of her batting his face with her tiny paws as he would open his mouth and play with her. Not once did he growl or get aggressive with her, even though she got a hook in him a few times. They would play often and then settle in on the dog bed next to the TV, snuggling next to one another. Occasionally, I would catch her trying to groom him by licking his head and face. It was adorable seeing how gentle he was with her. Every encounter with other animals was the same. He got along with everyone.

*Playing with Isabella*

*Napping with Isabella*

Moose's first play date was with an adorable Black Lab named Molly. Molly's parents were our good friends Jaxon and Tammy who had just started dating. They played tug of war and ran around the backyard together. Ginger just hung out in the room being a grumpy old lady. This first play date solidified his personality as being social with not just humans but also guests of the canine variety. They concluded their visit with a nap on the cool tile floor, but this wouldn't be Moose's only encounter with other dogs.

*His first play date with Molly*

My sister-in-law, Stephanie, was stationed in Waco with her husband at the time and would occasionally come up to Oklahoma City with their Jack Russell, Pistol. His name was a perfect fit for his personality since he was fast and spunky. At first, he and Moose would circle around, sniffing one another, but soon became good friends. They would run around the backyard chasing each other as grumpy old Ginger would just watch as if she was thinking to herself, "Those damn kids!" Playtime for Moose and Pistol continued in the house with a game of tug of war. Moose outweighed Pistol at least three times over, but he was so gentle with his new buddy. He had the strength to easily rip the rope out of Pistol's mouth or pull him across the floor, but he did neither. He patiently let Pistol tug at the rope with all his might before letting go of it. Pistol pranced around the house in victory as Moose watched him. It was almost as if a big brother would watch his little brother after letting him win at a video game. Occasionally, Moose would not realize his size, though.

One long weekend, we took a trip to see Odie's other sister, Margaret, who lived in Independence, Missouri, with her husband, Hector. They had a Shih Tzu named Shaggy, who was quite the character. He stole bacon right out of my hand once, and Hector thought it was hilarious. I couldn't hide my face, which showed I was less than amused. Margaret still tells that story, but Shaggy was about to get payback.

He got along fine with Moose and Ginger, but there was a chain link fence at the back of their property. The neighboring dogs loved to instigate. Well, instigate they did. They got all three of our dogs riled up and running back and forth. Moose and Ginger could keep pace with the neighboring dogs, but Shaggy got left behind on the first pass. When Moose and Ginger turned to go the opposite direction, Shaggy was trampled. He would get knocked down in the leaves and try to get up, only to be knocked down again. Margaret was freaking out, calling to Hector, "Babe! Babe! Shaggy!" I could hear the dogs barking and went out the back to see what was causing the ruckus. Shaggy was getting tossed around like a rag doll in the leaves. I hollered at my pups to come. They immediately stopped and came to the house with Shaggy in tow, covered in leaves. He was a little shaken up but luckily uninjured. Needless to say, I was amused. In all truth and honesty, Shaggy was a great dog and a long-term member of the family as a whole. We all miss his spunkiness, but I still guard my bacon with my life.

Continuing the trend of other family dogs, Odie has another sister, Judy (Odie's the oldest of six: four other sisters and one brother), who lives with her husband, Carlos, in El Paso, Texas. They have a nice home with a huge back porch and an above-ground pool, so visiting them is always a big hit with the kids. In true family fashion, we packed up the kids and the dogs and headed to El Paso in the SUV. We only had room for one kennel in the cargo space, so Ginger would ride in the kennel while Moose got to sit in the seat. Part of the reason was that Ginger's hair was hard to clean, but I think the reality is that Moose was a spoiled brat.

Judy and Carlos had two dogs. Brutus, a Bull Terrier mix, and Peanut, a Dachshund. Peanut was Carlos' baby but didn't get along with much of anyone else, including Brutus and Judy. Ginger had a history of not getting along with some dogs, so we kept her in a separate room. Moose was a different story since I knew he wouldn't get aggressive. As soon as we introduced Moose to Peanut, Peanut began barking at him and came right at him. Moose was terrified of the little guy and was doing everything he could to get away from Peanut. He ran right into the corner of a glass coffee table and got a cut under his eye before Carlos could grab Peanut and stop the chaos. I examined Moose and determined he would live without needing to be taken to the vet. Peanut eventually calmed down and Moose was able to roam free unmolested. We had many more visits with family, but one topic always persisted: how good of a boy Moose was. Carlos jokingly suggested a trade between Moose and Brutus, an offer which I immediately refused.

Being stationed in Oklahoma was great because both sets of grandparents lived an hour and a half away in my hometown. Their houses were a stone's throw from each other, so we would get to visit them often. Mommom Earlene and Papa Al, my mother's parents, owned a farm-style house on two acres, and we would usually stay with them. They had a female Brittany mix named Squirt since she peed when she got excited. Squirt was a runner, and the only person who could retrieve her was my cousin Miranda. I've already established that Moose was trained to come when called, but my grandmother had to use desperate means with Squirt. Her solution was to put her harness on her and tie a short log to the harness to keep her from being able to run too fast. I always felt a little guilty when Moose would take off in a dead run in the back pasture with Squirt following behind, encumbered by a piece of lumber. It was a good exercise for her, and she never got tangled or hurt.

My dad's parents, Grandma Bonnie and Papa Gene lived further south on Ranch Drive. When they passed, we purchased the home as a getaway cabin, but they also had two acres. Grandma Bonnie did not believe in dogs being indoors or on the furniture – part of the reason we would stay at Mommom's house. Papa Gene would occasionally get a hunting dog, but the dog wasn't part of the family. It had a purpose. This is not to say my grandfather wasn't a compassionate man. He was just a little old school. On one occasion, we took the kids and Moose in the SUV to their house. I let Moose out, and he sniffed Papa, staying close to the car. I told Moose to go play and pointed to the pasture. He bolted, enjoying the warm summer air and the sunshine in an open field. I let him explore the perimeter of the property before saying, "Come here, boy!" as I clapped three times. He looked up from whatever he was sniffing and made a beeline to me. My grandfather looked at him and then at me before he said with a country accent, "Jake, that dog sure does mind good." Moose got to go in the house that day, but I realized that other people's opinions about dogs were influencing our actions but were sometimes displaced.

One such occasion was when we had company over, and a guest noticed he was sitting next to the coffee table drooling as we were eating. This person made the request that we put him away while we were eating. He wasn't stealing food or trying to lick peoples' plates, but I succumbed to the pressure to put him away in the room. I felt a pang of guilt when I ushered him to the bedroom and put him away. I'll never forget the sad look on his face as I closed the door. I'm sure he was wondering what he did wrong. The fact of the matter is he had done nothing wrong. It was his house and our guest had overstepped a boundary. I vowed that day that I would never let "opinions" determine how I would treat my dog whose importance to my family surpassed human pettiness. In fact, his emotional intelligence surpassed most if not all human instinct. He was a highly intelligent being who actually had some serious Houdini skills which are evident in retrospect in telling his story.

One such escape happened at a squadron picnic on Tinker Air Force Base. It was a beautiful day, and everyone was encouraged to bring their pups. I went by myself and showed face because Odie and the kids were engaged in some other activity. I loaded Moose into the truck with his blue harness and set out for the festivities. I found my buddy Tony and we found a place at a picnic table to sit and discuss how class was going. You know typical chop talk. I didn't want to hang on to Moose's leash, so I tethered him to a table leg feeling confident he was sufficiently detained. I got up to get a burger and a coke and returned to the discussion. I was in mid-sentence when Tony grinned and pointed to where Moose was tethered. I had a mild panic attack when I saw an empty harness. Then Tony pointed behind me. There was Moose wagging his tail and looking up at me. Apparently, he had lifted each leg up out of the harness and freed himself from captivity because he wasn't comfortable with me being gone. This would not be the last time Tony would take part in his antics. No, there was one occasion where he didn't come back and gave Odie and I quite a scare.

Odie and I would frequently host Super Bowl parties and other get togethers at our house. We would let Moose and Ginger run free in the house for the most part. On one occasion, we had a guest with a little boy who was fiddling with the gate to the backyard and left it open. I didn't know about this until after most everyone had left. My buddy Tony and I were sitting in the garage wrapping up the festivities when he said, "Ginger and Moose just ran past." I immediately got up and hollered for them, but Moose's loyalty tied him to his sister, and he just wasn't listening. It was dark, and we tried to follow them on foot, but we couldn't see them. I got in the SUV with Tony, and we drove around the neighborhood. Nothing. I was getting worried. I told Tony he didn't need to stay with me all night, so he left sometime after midnight.

I continued to search for them outside our neighborhood to the south in an open field in the dark with the headlights and a flashlight. It had rained the day prior, so the field was muddy. I knew that I couldn't stop, or I might get stuck. So, what did I do? I stopped. The SUV was stuck. I got out in the mud and examined the back tire, which had been spinning in the mud. My dogs were gone, and now I had got my wife's SUV stuck in the mud at one o'clock in the morning. I got back in and gave one last-ditch effort to free up the tank in low gear. I got her out. Knowing that the darkness was going to prevent an effective search, I returned home and slept in the cab of my project truck with the garage door open in case they came back. I didn't sleep well at all, impatiently waiting for the sun to rise. It rose about seven in the morning.

I came into the house and took a shower to wake up before hopping in my daily driver truck to search for them. They were both chipped, but like an idiot, I had never set up the website. I was panicking. I decided to start driving north through an adjacent housing area. I was driving slowly and had my eyes peeled for my precious fur babies. I made it through the neighborhood and came to a major crossroad almost a mile north of our house. Not a car was on the road. I was about to turn left, but something told me to turn right. I'm not sure what it was exactly, but it was a feeling compelling me to not go left. So, I turned right on the major road, fearing that I would find them injured in the street, hit by a car, or worse. I passed some trees on the left side of the road, which opened my field of view into an open field. I saw two tails poking up from the tall grass. I stopped in the middle of the street, rolled down the window, and hollered, "Moose! Ginger!" Moose was the first to react. He raised his head out of the field and barked once. I told them to "Get over here!" They both came immediately and jumped in the truck. I had them back.

On the way home, I called Odie crying. I just told her, "I found them, Babe! I found them!" It was a short trip back to the house, and they acted like nothing happened. I was honestly a little angry with them. It was like when a parent loses their kid in the mall. You are relieved, but then you get mad at them for wandering. We pulled into the driveway, and I let Moose out first. I had a strong hold on Ginger's collar and the scruff of her neck as we entered the house. They were exhausted and dirty from roaming the streets all night. They needed a bath badly, but I just let them collapse on their beds in the living room to sleep. Mom and Dad took a nap. I don't think I have ever been that distraught, but they were safe and back home.

Moose was fiercely loyal and didn't leave Ginger's side that whole night, but he had a few little quirks as well. Two come to mind as funny things he would do. The first one was back massages. He would sit down with his back to Odie, turn his head around, and stare at her until she would give him a back massage. He never asked me to give him one. I'm not sure why, but it seemed to me that he loved Odie in a different way. I was a good-time dad and the disciplinarian, a role I don't remember assuming more than once or twice. Mom, on the other hand, was the nurturing one. She would take him in the room for nap time, and they developed a different bond than that which existed between him and me. So, she got the privilege of giving him massages...and dancing with him.

It was an odd thing to see my wife dancing with such a handsome boy and giving me a slight twinge of jealousy. I suppose I deserved it since before we started dating, we were on military business in Las Vegas and had gone out to a club. Odie asked me to dance, and I declined. I've never lived that down, so here was my comeuppance. She would be watching TV and a song from a commercial would begin to play. She would begin stepping to the tune and look at him. If he was lying down, he would immediately get up and start wagging his tail in anxious anticipation of what he knew was about to happen. He would get closer and look up at her waiting for the signal. He was never a dog that jumped on people so he would wait for the green light symbolized by her tapping on her shoulders with her hands. He would jump up and put his paws on her shoulders as they would dance around the living room. The funny thing was that he never wanted to dance with me. It was a special event reserved only for Mom.

My special event was rubbing his ears. I mentioned earlier that a Labrador's ears are the softest material known to man. They were irresistible. I was the only one who could stick my thumbs on both sides and dig deep until he groaned with contentment. It wasn't because he was unwilling to do it, but because Odie was always grossed out by it. She refused to touch the insides of his ears and always scolded me if I didn't wash my hands afterward. I'll admit that there were times that Moose and I would be hanging out when Odie wasn't watching, and I didn't wash my hands. That was a secret between my buddy and me.

Another funny quirk occurred because of his persistent habit of following me around. Our kitchen has a door that leads to the laundry room where the staircase for our loft is. I'm constantly going up and down the stairs to get another beer or to let the dogs out. Moose would occasionally get trapped in there. The first sign that he was trapped was him putting his paws on the floor and pushing them under the door. He would sit there for several minutes in hopes that someone would see his feet and rescue him. Usually, I would remember he got trapped and rescue him within minutes, but if he felt like help wasn't coming, he would let out a single bark. Yep, one bark. That's how we knew he was stuck. He'd wait patiently by the door until we would open it and he could join in on whatever festivities were occurring with the family.

Sometimes his shadowy tendencies could get a little annoying, but he was so darn cute and loveable that the annoyance never really took hold. One weekend Mommom and Papa Al came to visit us so my grandfather could "help" me build a shed. His idea of helping was to sit on a chair, sipping lemonade and questioning everything I was doing. Don't get me wrong he knew exactly what he was doing, and it was all in good fun. I cherish those moments with him especially since he had his own nickname for Moose like he did for me. My term of address was "Jaker," while Moose's was "Moosie Goosie." Well, Moosie Goosie was still a pup and followed me around everywhere I went. I was always afraid of dropping a hammer on him or stepping on him. Do you know how hard it is to get a shed square with a puppy at your feet and an ornery old fellow asking you why you predrilled with screws instead of using nails? Let me tell you, it was a challenge, but we got the job complete and that shed is still standing...screws and all.

Moose was as patient as any living creature could be and had a sensitive side. One day I came home from work and Chelsey had a sheepish grin on her face. I was curious as to whether Odie had bought her something frivolous or she experienced some trouble from school. I asked why she was grinning, and she just eyeballed Moose who was sitting all majestically and gazing up at me satisfied with his daily greeting. It was then that I noticed his paws. They were different somehow, and after a closer examination, I realized his claws had been painted with nail polish. Apparently, my daughter had taken my tough and handsome "hunting" dog and emasculated him by painting his toenails. Odie then informed me that he had sat ever so gently while Chelsey applied nail polish to his claws. I couldn't help but laugh recognizing the irony behind that Labradors are bred to be tough and resilient to weather to retrieve game from the wild in austere conditions. This situation was the antithesis of the stereotype and Moose had broken the glass ceiling of what was normally accepted for his breed.

Another occasion of how he wasn't the toughest guy happened on a trip to see Odie's mother in El Paso.

Like his "toughness" displayed while inadvertently trampling poor Shaggy, he decided to confront the neighbor's dog. There was a stone wall about four to five feet high separating the back yards and there was a dog next door that would lose it every time someone came outside. He would bark ferociously and jump high enough where we could see his head. Moose naturally wanted to exert his dominance as well, but failed to realize the nature of the south Texas desert was highly inhospitable. He discovered "stickers" in the soil and upon lodging one in his paw, immediately limped back to the door from which I had released him into the desert environment. It was a pitiful sight to see. He whimpered as he sought comfort from Dad, and after close examination, I removed the thorn from the "lion's" paw. After that significant emotional event. He trod lightly in the backyard and stayed in the air conditioning for the rest of the trip. This was another of many of Moose's idiosyncrasies.

There were also a few things that Moose didn't like. One was having people look him in the eyes or touch his face. He would always turn away if you looked him in the eyes and if you tried to pull his face toward you, he would pull away. Moose wasn't the type of dog that gave puppy kisses. When I would come home from work, his method of showing affection was to rub up against you, but he disliked having his face touched. His soft ears and loving face were irresistible! To have a dog so lovable who resisted touch to his face was inconceivable. I can only chalk this up to his submissive nature. Dogs who have strong personalities won't hesitate to look you in the eye, but Moose was different. He had a non-confrontational character in his DNA that suppressed aggression and conflict.

Moose also disliked conflict which was easily recognizable by his behavior. In any household where humans reside, there is always a level of tension that sometimes leads to verbal conflict. Humans are creatures of chaos and Moose would exhibit signs of distress when the harmony was disrupted in our house. If an argument broke out between the fallible personalities of the humans in his pack, he would retreat to a quiet place until the storm blew over. He could not handle disharmony and would lay next to a closed door until we realized that he was highly uncomfortable. He had a way of bringing peace to turmoil which created an aura that permeated through the house with a calming effect. Whatever disagreement took place was often resolved by reading his body language. It became commonplace to read his mood. If Moose was acting in a reclusive manner, we recognized that he internalized the friction which ultimately made us better at resolving conflicts. Sometimes his discomfort would have to take a second seat to cuteness and photo opportunities.

These photo opportunities would be personified around a favorite holiday – Halloween. When a couple is nearing the end of parenthood and facing the ominous situation of being empty nesters, the pets often suffer abhorrible atrocities. When the teenagers are embarrassed by the innocence of traditions, the pets suffer the horrific transference of these traditions. With Moose, it was Halloween costumes. Odie and I could not resist the urge to dress him up in any and all ridiculous costumes the major retail stores offered. Normally I am opposed to the commercial shenanigans centered around holidays, but in this case, it was completely justified. Moose was subjugated to the embarrassment of being a lobster, a frog, a bunch of grapes, and the worst of all...the impersonation of a bull with a stuffed bull rider holding a simulated saddle in one hand and a hat in the other raised above his head with an embedded wire. He hated every moment of being outfitted with a costume. Moose would lay his ears down and his tail would cease to wag. His tail would extend parallel to the ground away from the cheap fabric pressed against his beautiful waxy Labrador coat. He suffered in silence but always played along as if he knew how much seeing him in ridiculous costumes brought the rest of us so much joy. His tolerance would soon be tested by another member of the family, not of the furry persuasion.

*Halloween costumes with Ginger and Isabella*

Our son Kyle learned as he graduated basic training in the Air Force that he was having a child, and the shotgun wedding was taking place the same weekend. Yes, his soon to be wife, Caroline, had hidden the fact she was carrying our grandson Karmine from him to prevent Kyle from making a rash decision and withdrawing. You're probably wondering what the back story is here, but this work is about Moose and not my grandkids. That narrative would be exponentially longer and an incomplete work since we have four grandkids now whose lives are just beginning. So, I'll table that for now and continue with Moose's story of being an "Uncle" to baby Karmine.

Moose's gentility was even more solidified when Karmine was born. The birth was a C-section, and we were so joyous to have a new addition to the family. Odie and I were grandparents which is a game-changer. Kyle was attending training and Caroline was still holding down a job to make ends meet like all young couples strive to do. Caroline spent a lot of time in our house during the pregnancy and started to develop a bond with Moose. Animals are highly in tune with human physiology, so it was no surprise that when Odie agreed to set up "Nana daycare" with Karmine, Moose became a companion to him. As an infant, Karmine would begin to nurture his connection with dogs. Moose sniffed him curiously at first and then began to lay his head on Karmine's bouncer as the tiny human would sleep.

As Karmine grew older and began to develop a personality, my experiences upon returning home from work became an even more joyous highlight of the day. I was not only greeted by Moose, but now I had a smiling child as well. Odie and I tried to have our own kids, but it wasn't in the cards, so I was seeing for the first time how much of a role pets play with babies. Older siblings are often resistant to a new addition to the family due to jealousy, but Moose seemed to feed spiritually on new life. A bond began to develop between Karmine and Moose that would last for over ten years.

*Protecting Karmine*

Once Karmine became mobile and began to crawl, we set up an area in the living room that kept him contained. Ginger and Moose could enter the "cage" freely, but Ginger would keep her distance for the most part. Moose on the other hand seemed to be drawn to the little guy. On Karmine's first birthday, someone thought it would be a good idea to get him a baby drum set with baby drumsticks. Moose eventually became the drum and patiently laid on the floor as Karmine practiced his musical skills on Moose's haunches. That precious being never budged. He would lay there as Karmine would whack him with drumsticks, crawl over top of him, and tug at his ears. Some would say we gave Karmine too much leeway and risked his safety, but Odie and I knew better. Moose was one hundred and one percent trustworthy.

When Karmine began to walk, Moose became the concerned parent and would investigate every time Karmine would fall. If Karmine was crying, Moose's uncomfortable behavior would manifest. He disliked the commotion and would follow Karmine around as the adults would console him, feed him, or change his diaper. Moose was intimately involved in all aspects of Karmine's life and showed genuine concern for the well-being of his "nephew." We even began calling our beloved dog "Uncle Moose."

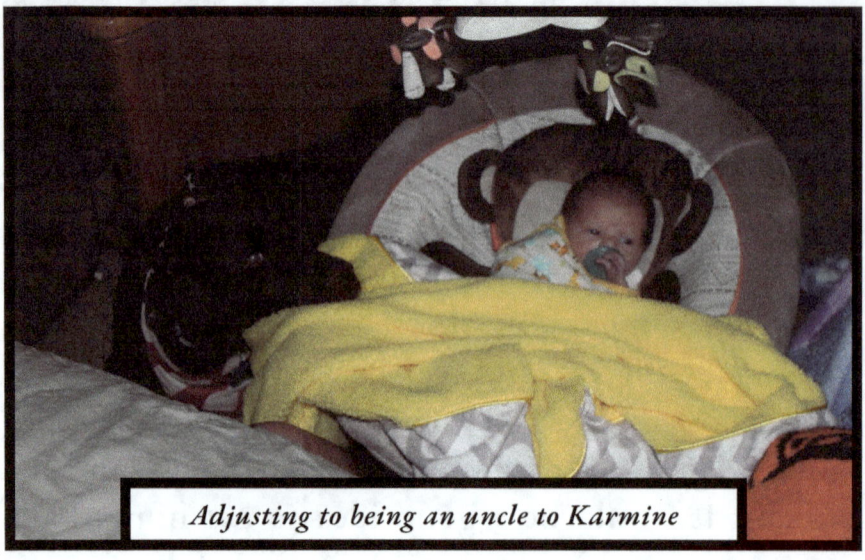

*Adjusting to being an uncle to Karmine*

Karmine turned two and Odie and I were faced with the inevitable reality that I was about to face a permanent change of station, or a "PCS" as we call it in the military. Odie had been stationed overseas in England, but I was fifteen years in and had only been CONUS (continental United States). She was yearning for a new adventure, so I requested an assignment in Germany. My commander at the time worked with us to delay our move so Chelsey could graduate high school and we began preparation to make our trek to Germany with Ginger, Moose, and Isabella. Thus, opened an exciting new challenge. Chelsey agreed that a three-year tour to Europe was palatable since she contracted the travel bug through a band trip to England a few years prior. We settled on the decision that we would rent our house and I would go first to "prepare the battlespace." Odie and Chelsey would face the arduous task of transporting themselves and three animals from the United States to Germany on top of preparing the house for movers, cleaning the house for renters, and planning the transportation to Dallas for an overseas flight.

# CHAPTER 3:

# THE EUROPEAN ADVENTURE

I did everything in my power to prepare Odie and Chelsey for the journey ahead. Chelsey was about to graduate high school and would accompany us on our journey to Germany. I began to research the methods by which we would travel with Ginger, Moose, and Isabella across the Atlantic. Luckily, I had some great friends, Brad and Katie, who departed with their two large dogs in March 2015. Their advice was invaluable as we prepped for the next adventure. The first step was to procure plane tickets.

We had two options. The first was to attempt to get rotator slots with our pets. The rotator is a government contracted method of travel reserved for military family members moving overseas. I contacted the base agency that runs the program, and they were about as helpful as a screen door on a submarine. The Air Force has made leaps and bounds in improving the program for traveling with pets, but in 2015, the process was a huge hassle and very restrictive. I couldn't do anything until I had official orders, and even if they could get spots, the limit was two pets per family, and we had three. Their advice (my second option) was to get permission to travel "circuitously," which meant that we would need to procure the tickets ourselves which gave me more flexibility for traveling from Oklahoma City. I completed the paperwork for circuitous travel and began exploring the options.

I found a U.S. carrier that was partnered with the German company Lufthansa who is known for being very caring with animals on their flights. The trouble was that the nearest international airport was in Dallas, Fort Worth. I talked with Odie, and we agreed that would be our best option. It was a direct flight to Frankfurt, Germany, so we would need to figure out the ground transportation from Oklahoma City to Dallas and from Frankfurt to Spangdahlem. The cost of the tickets was comparable to what the government would pay for circuitous travel, and the cost of the pets was based on their size. Isabella's airfare was $200, while each of the dogs was $400. I considered that an easy cost of $1000, so I made the reservations for Chelsey and Odie to fly out in October.

My report date was July, and we had to prep the house for renters. I would leave before the Fourth of July weekend and prepare the battlespace for the remainder of our family to arrive in early October. Odie would stay behind with Chelsey and prepare the house. I arranged for our household goods to be picked up in enough time to get them delivered to Germany before Odie and Chelsey would arrive. We also decided to ship my truck, which I had bought a few years earlier. Odie moved in with Caroline and Kyle who had already graduated basic training and was working on base as a maintenance crew chief on the E-3 Sentry – the command-and-control platform on which I had been flying for the last five years. I deployed twice for six months during that time, and Kyle deployed once. Having family in town greatly decreased the cost of the delayed move for Odie and Chelsey.

In early July of 2015, I flew out for my first trip to Europe since 1999 when I was part of Operation Allied Force. I arranged for travel from Frankfort to Spangdahlem with the base shuttle and remember the driver talking incessantly while I was intrigued but fighting to stay awake after my intercontinental flight. Brad and Katie were great hosts when I arrived, and I was so thankful for them. They had a spare bedroom in the basement of their house in Grosslittgen, where I stayed. I had a room on base, but it was on a high floor in the billeting building. The heat that July was setting records and the first night I stayed there, I sweat the whole night. Central air conditioning isn't a thing in Europe, so having a cool basement in which to sleep was literally a breath of fresh air. They let me borrow their second car until I was able to procure a form of transportation. I found a good deal on an Audi A6 Avant station wagon, which I bought from an expatriate from the States. The cargo space was perfect for the dogs, and the two-liter turbo diesel drove so nicely on the autobahn. The next step was housing.

The housing office at Spangdahlem was amazing, but having pets narrowed my options. I really loved the little village of Grosslittgen and found a large two-story house with four bedrooms and an attached garage not more than three blocks from Brad and Katie. I called the people who owned the house, and they answered, speaking German. In broken German, I asked if someone spoke English. A young male came on the phone and translated for me. I arranged a viewing, and as we hung up, I swore I heard them speaking Russian. I noticed that the lady's name on the paperwork was Irina, which was not a German name. It's important to note here that I was a Russian Linguist before I was commissioned, a skill that would be instrumental in ensuring we had a good home for the pets.

I drove to the house and the door was cracked open. I entered and said, "Allo?" the German form of greeting. Irina was upstairs cleaning and came down the steps right next to the front door. She immediately started speaking to me in German to which I responded that I did not speak German. This was my chance to take a huge risk. I asked her in Russian if she spoke Russian since I didn't speak English. Her face lit up, and we immediately began speaking Russian. She informed me that she was indeed ethnic Russian and had moved to Germany with her husband shortly after the Soviet Union collapsed. I have never heard a person talk so quickly and it was difficult to keep up. She showed me around the house, which was spacious and perfect for our needs since it had a backyard. This was when I turned on the charm and showed her pictures of my "sobaki" Ginger and Moose. I assured her they were good pups and would not do any damage to her beautiful home. We sealed the deal, and I moved into an empty house in Germany a week later. I honestly think that speaking Irina's native tongue was the only reason she agreed to let us have our pets.

The plan for our household goods went perfectly. I was able to unpack all the boxes and set up the house well before Odie and Chelsey were scheduled to arrive. I was in a holding pattern waiting for them to arrive, constantly worrying about them since I could not help them. In the meantime, they were preparing for the flight of a lifetime. In the Air Force, we have a term called "force ratio," which drives a fighter pilot's tactics. If the fight is four good guys against eight bad guys, the tactics are significantly different than four good guys against two bad guys. Odie and Chelsey were not winning from a force ratio standpoint, with two humans carrying three pets, four checked bags, and two carry-ons. They hit some snags along the way, but they pulled it off.

Odie rented a van for ground transportation from Oklahoma City to the Dallas Fort Worth airport. She dropped off the van and used the airport shuttle to transport five living beings to the hotel, which was conveniently located near the airport. They settled in and went to bed early, knowing that the next morning would be a meat grinder. This was when the first snag occurred. The kennel requirement for overseas travel was to have metal bolts and nuts in every hole, attaching the bottom half to the top half. I knew this back in June and bought the correct bolts for Odie. In her defense, she had a lot going on those three months, but she forgot the hardware.

The shuttle only made runs to and from the airport, so she was forced to call a cab. Luckily, she found a cab that was willing to wait for her. She tried a couple of stores and finally found one with the required nuts and bolts. She retrieved the bolts and returned to the hotel to assemble the kennels. Odie is great when it comes to timings. She had built in enough flexibility that she was still on time to check in. That was when she hit her second snag. The shuttle was full.

Frantic to find transportation for the luggage, three kennels, and two adults, Odie reached out to the front desk. One of the hotel employees offered to give her a ride and she made it to the airport in time to process the paperwork and board. The first big obstacle was overcome, so now I was waiting to finalize the trip from Frankfurt to our house.

Quick pause here to address the nature of humanity. We have all been in situations that are desperate and dire. I'm a huge proponent of karma, and I truly believe that we should all pay it forward. It's always easy to assume that other people's problems are not ours, but in moments of true need, there are people who understand the context and often make those little strides that can really help their fellow humans out. I don't know where the cab driver or the hotel employee are now, but their patience and kindness will never be forgotten. I hope they are living fulfilling lives and reflect fondly on how their willingness to help my family was a godsend.

Odie and I were in close communication throughout the process of boarding the plane. I wish I could say I was patient, but I'll admit that I was highly frustrated that Odie forgot the hardware. It reminds me of the scene in Pulp Fiction when Bruce Willis' character was upset with his girlfriend for forgetting his father's watch. We moved past it, though, and pressed with the next step.

I coordinated with the base to arrange travel from Frankfurt to the base in the same van that I was on a few months before. I knew they would need help at the airport, so I drove the Audi to the airport and parked it in temporary parking. I knew we would not be able to fit all the luggage in the Audi, so the van would fulfill that purpose. As I was eagerly waiting in the airport, I ensured the van was there and ready before proceeding to the luggage claim section of the terminal. I received a text from Odie saying that they had arrived. I did not know that the fees for processing Moose, Ginger, and Isabella had to be paid in Euros, so when she began processing the paperwork (a very extensive process that begins months before departure), she had to find an ATM to retrieve the cash.

After what seemed like an eternity, I finally saw them walking with all the luggage toward me. My feelings were a mixture of relief that they had arrived safely, guilt that I had not been there to help them, and joy for seeing them for the first time in months. The fur babies were in good health and seemed very relaxed, considering the long day they had experienced. The force ratio was now even, and we started to arrange for the travel plan back to base.

My plan was to break down the dog kennels and put them in the van with the luggage. We had paid for the transportation of the pets and two passengers, but the driver was the same guy as before. I felt safer with my living cargo with me so I told the guy that I would meet him at the base to unload our luggage. As we waited for some of the other passengers to arrive and board the van, we took Moose and Ginger out to use the bathroom on the way to temporary parking. Moose and Ginger got settled in the back of the Audi, and Chelsey took the back seat with Isabella still in her kennel. Odie sat in the front seat, and we set out to our new home.

The feelings of stress subsided as excitement rolled in. The two-hour trip was ripe with conversations about how complicated the process was, how neat the house would be to live in, how well the Audi drove, and the beauty of Germany. I could tell all five of them were exhausted, and I prepped the beds for them in anticipation. I drove directly to the house as we unloaded the pets and introduced them to their new home. Isabella went straight to the litter box, and the pups went straight to their water bowls. After the pets finished fulfilling their anatomical needs, I ushered Chelsey upstairs to her "room." The house was so big that she, in essence, had her own apartment upstairs with a room, a living area, a bathroom, and access to a balcony overlooking the backyard. Ginger was really her dog, so she followed immediately up the stairs with Chelsey.

After showing them around, I stopped and noticed Moose and Isabella weren't with us. I figured Isabella was doing her own exploring, but it seemed odd that Moose didn't follow behind. I called for him and he didn't come, which was out of character and caused me to get concerned. I went back down the stairs and saw him at the bottom of the stairs with his tail wagging. I urged him to come up the stairs, and he hesitated with his glance shifting from me to the first stair and then back to me. He put his paw on the first stair and then back on the floor. I thought this was strange since he never had issues going up the stairs in the house in Oklahoma. Was he injured? That's when it hit me. The stairs in the German house were solid granite suspended by a metal frame with gaps between the steps. He was afraid of the gaps. I didn't force him to come up, and it never became an issue since he would end up hanging out with us downstairs for the duration of our stay. We had loved Moose for over six years, and we were still learning about the quirks of his personality.

My family was finally here and settled into our home. I kissed Odie and told her I would be back with the luggage. I proceeded to the base and parked at the billeting parking lot. As I entered, I was pleased to see all our luggage and the kennels stacked nicely and neatly in the corner of the lobby, as I had requested. I loaded up the bags in my truck, which had arrived a few weeks earlier. As I returned, I found all five of my family members crashed and snuggled into their beds. I unloaded the luggage, and just left it in the foyer. I walked into the kitchen and opened the tiny European fridge whose contents resembled my life of bachelorhood for the last few months. I reached for a Dunkel beer and poured it into my glass that came with the crate of beer. As I sat on the couch and turned on my video games, I sighed with a breath of relief as I took my first sip of pure contentedness. Mission complete.

The next day was set aside for getting cell phones and coordinating driver's licenses. That all went well, with nothing significant to report. Also on the agenda was a trip to Stuttgart for Oktoberfest which I arranged through a friend at work. Odie and Chelsey were apprehensive about attending such an event three days after arriving, but we agreed we would take every opportunity to experience what Europe had to offer. I arranged to have Moose and Ginger

*Running with Ginger at the kennel at Spangdahlem Air Base, Germany.*

boarded at the kennel on base for three days while we went to Oktoberfest. We felt guilty after abandoning them so soon after they arrived, but the staff was very receptive and helped to ease our angst. The cover photo of Moose on the front of the book is courtesy of the staff at the Spangdahlem Air Base kennel. They took great care of our pups, and we would take advantage of their services many times during our stay in Germany.

The house was great, but the only downfall was that there was no fence. I anticipated this, so I fixed a cable tether for Ginger that was just long enough to give her plenty of room to roam in the backyard but could still reach the back door. Moose would just wander and occasionally trip over her tether. I would let him outside the back door only to find him at the front door or coming to see me in the garage. The garage had three entrances: one at the front with a large door like what you would see in the States, one leading to the house, and one leading to the backyard. The door to the backyard had a grate in front of it, and Moose would refuse to cross it. He would walk all the way around the house and enter through the main garage door. Never figured out why he was so afraid of that grate.

The front door to the house was heavy and had a strong German-built latch with a stiff spring. It required a bit more force to close than American doors. One day, I apparently did not close it properly. This was brought to my attention while Odie and Chelsey were on an outing in the local town of Trier, which had a beautiful downtown ideal for Christmas markets. I had been there before and wasn't keen on the idea of waiting outside store after store as they shopped. So, I elected to stay home and play video games (seeing a trend here?). I was interrupted by the obnoxious sound of the doorbell, which resembled the sound of a prank hand buzzer amplified ten-fold. I was greeted by a little German boy about ten years old. With a thick German accent, he asked me politely, "Do you have two dogs?" I replied, "Yes," with curiosity as to why he was asking. He then said, "Zey are running in ze field." They had escaped again! Luckily, this time, I had this little boy and his friends who helped me corral Ginger and get both her and Moose back to the house.

That field across from our house was an extra playground for not just our pups but also for Brad and Katie's pups. Mia and Nike would often link up with Moose and Ginger for walks around the village. As already established, Moose could be trusted off-

*Playing in the fields by the house in Grosslittgen, Germany.*

leash, and we would let him roam through the fields. He would hop up and down, appearing and disappearing into and out of the tall grass. The backyard was also a perfect space for fetch. Ironically, we had a tennis court behind our backyard which would frequently supply Moose with additional balls. I don't think I bought a single ball while in Germany.

*Playing fetch at the kennel at*
*Spangdahlem Air Base, Germany*

We traveled quite a bit while in Germany, but mostly one-day trips since there was so much to see. If we did stay overnight, we would board the pups at either the base kennel or with an older couple in our village who had a large pasture that was fenced in. The thing about Europe is that you see dogs everywhere. The only real limitation is the grocery stores, but restaurants and retail stores are all fair game. We would often take Moose and Ginger with us on our outings, and they were very rarely ever shunned. Usually, the locals would welcome them with treats and pets.

We were somewhat limited in our travels while in Germany because my unit was gearing up for a six-month deployment to the Middle East. Odie and Chelsey didn't arrive until late September, and we were slated for an April departure. Granted, that was a six-month span, but we had exercises and "spin-up" events leading up to the April deployment. Not to mention leave over the holidays which carries more weight when our military people are stationed overseas for three and four years at a time. I had plans to come back to the States and see Karmine, and Odie and Chelsey enjoyed the Christmas markets in Europe. Moose and Ginger would enjoy the German snowfall, and soon the year 2016 would arrive with only three months before deployment. Brad and I would depart together soon and become roommates for six months. We never shared a crossword on the whole deployment and our relationship was strengthened through tragedy. I don't know what I would have done if I hadn't had him there when our family suffered the loss of Ginger.

This book is about Moose, but I'd be remiss to exclude the story about Ginger's last few months because it provides a foundation for later chapters. I intentionally left out some details about the late summer of 2015. After I left in July, Chelsey noticed a lump on Ginger's lower jaw. Because we were so close to travel and the lump was so small, we decided to deal with it after the move. After Ginger arrived and over the course of a few months, we realized that we should have dealt with it earlier, but hindsight is 20/20. The lump grew over the course of about two months to the size of a shooter marble and soon it had grown to the size of a golf ball. It was time for action, albeit a little too late.

I researched a few vets in the local area since the Spangdahlem clinic didn't deal with major surgeries. It was too late to put her on an insurance plan since the condition was already present, but we immediately bought one for Moose, which would pay dividends in the future. We settled on a clinic that dealt with cancer surgery after the biopsy came back positive. We had three options. First was to do nothing and let the cancer run its course with an inevitable early end to Ginger's life. The second was to remove her entire lower jaw, expose possible infection, and severely decrease her quality of life. We went with the third option, which was to remove as much of the tumor as the surgeon could, but this option was low on the probability that all the cancerous tissue would be eradicated. The mitigation plan was chemotherapy.

We took her in for the surgery, and it went well. She was on pain medication that caused hallucinations, about which the doctor warned us, mentioning she would be seeing "pink bunnies." When we returned home, I carried her into the house and laid her on the floor with a blanket. The doctor wasn't wrong. She lay there crying and making strange noises as her legs wiggled furiously. It only lasted a day. She was up and around the next day and back to her old self. Bleeding was an issue, but her appetite was unaffected. She took her chemo treatments like a champ, and the tumor seemed to be stopped for a while but soon returned and continued to grow in the weeks before I deployed.

I left for the deployment and tearfully said goodbye to Ginger and the rest of the family to fulfill my obligations as a military member. Odie and I talked every day while I was deployed, and Ginger's condition worsened. She never lost her spirit, but the time came when she was bleeding horribly, and it was mixed with a disgusting discharge. Odie made the arrangements, and I was with her on video when it happened. I told Ginger I loved her as the doctor performed the euthanasia. Odie gasped because the death happened so quickly. Ginger was alert and coherent; then she wasn't. I heard Odie cry, "That was so fast!" as the three of us began sobbing. Ginger was 14 years old.

Like any military member, I pushed it down and proceeded with the rest of my day after telling Odie I loved her as she finished up the arrangements for cremation. Katie was there for Odie and Chelsey and naturally talked to Brad about it. I was asleep by the time Brad got back to the tiny room we stayed in. We both woke up at the same time together the next day to do the Lord's work. He asked me if I wanted to talk about it. Not wanting to show weakness, I quietly said, "No," but Brad knew better. He wrapped me in a hug as I let the tears fall. Everyone needs a friend like Brad.

The rest of the deployment was routine, with six days on and one day off. It was rigorous but very rewarding. "Kingpin" was our command-and-control callsign, and we were doing great things controlling aircraft in the Arabian Gulf, Afghanistan, Iraq, and Syria across 940,000 square miles of airspace. But all good things must come to an end, and the time to return was fast approaching. Odie was in the States when I returned home, and she had left Moose with the older couple in our village. Katie was kind enough to ensure my truck was drivable when we arrived on base. On an October afternoon, I cranked her up and set out to retrieve my buddy. He was so excited when I picked him up. His tail was wagging and taking his entire body with it. We got in the truck and drove the few blocks home. I turned the key and entered the house. Moose followed behind me and I sat on the step which he had tried to climb so many months earlier. The sounds and smells were familiar and comforting. I sat there sobbing for what seemed like hours, releasing the pain and welcoming the relief of being home at last. But the home was so empty.

The next day, my friend Teresa, whose callsign was "Dirty," offered to pick me up and drive me to her home to hang out with her family. She's always been a selfless person of high emotional intelligence and knew it would be rough for me to come home to an empty house. "Ditty" Dittman, Teresa's husband, was also deployed with us since they were a "mil-to-mil" couple. She promised homemade tortillas and beer, so I couldn't resist. We had a great time hanging out, and I enjoyed socializing with their two boys, Gabe and Chance. Ditty's brother, Michael, was also there and showed signs of relief as he was the boys' caretaker for six months while Teresa and Ditty were deployed. She and Gabe drove me home after I had my fill of beer and wonderful food. I'll always remember the camaraderie we had in the 606th Air Control Squadron.

But for now, I was back home in Germany with my buddy Moose. We slept with Isabella in the bedroom with the crazy wallpaper for a week or two until Chelsey and Odie returned from the States. It was a time of healing and bonding before our next adventure. My unit was tasked to move from Germany to Italy, and most of the work had already been done. I returned to the squadron after six months of deployment to a ghost town. All the equipment was gone, and we were a skeleton crew. Since my parents were coming to visit for Christmas and through the New Year, our family was one of the last to leave in mid-January on our trek south to Aviano Airbase, Italy.

I sent my parents back to the States, and we began our preparations to travel across Europe with Moose and Isabella. It was January, so snow was a high probability, knowing we would have to cross the Alps. I had my full-size Chevy four-by-four, and the Audi was all-wheel drive, so we were well equipped for what the weather might hold. The movers came to pack up all the stuff we weren't taking with us in the cars, and we moved into temporary lodging on base for about a week while I finished up the out-processing paperwork. The temporary lodging on Spangdahlem Air Base was surprisingly comfortable since it was basically a three-bedroom furnished apartment. The only catch was it was on the second story and the steps were the same type as the ones in the house. No amount of coaxing could get Moose to go up or down those darn stairs, so for about a week, Chelsey and I had to carry him up and down those steps. If you remember what I said earlier about the force ratio, it was in our favor since we had three humans to two animals now.

Once I had my final appointment, we were ready to hit the road. We agreed the logical division of passengers would be girls vs. boys. Odie and Chelsey crammed Isabella into her kennel and loaded up in the Audi. I took Moose in the truck with me. I placed the luggage on the floorboard on the passenger side to level off the top of the seat and then placed a comforter over the luggage and seat so he could have more space to get comfortable. The journey was ominous but having Moose by my side made it so much less stressful. I remember as we set off on the autobahn how ironic it was that I was traveling across Europe in one of the most iconic American vehicles imaginable with a Labrador in the passenger seat. It doesn't get much more red-blooded 'Merican than that. Did I mention I was also wearing a camouflage Chevy ball cap? I think you get the idea.

So, we hit the road on our next journey. I was in the lead, and Chelsey was driving the Audi. We agreed the trip could be done in two days and had arranged to stay at the same hotel, Brad and Katie had used in a small town in Austria. Brad and Katie stayed there with Mia and Nike in November when they drove down to Aviano. They have great taste so we knew we would be comfortable. It snowed both days of travel, but the first day was uneventful. We made frequent stops and fueled up. This was the first time we had paid full European prices for gas since we always bought at a discount on base. I think it was upwards of 200 Euros to fill up my truck. It didn't matter though because we were going to live in Italy!

We arrived at the pet-friendly hotel, and the parking lot was covered in snow. I swapped out my ball cap for a stocking cap as Moose started to stir after his long nap time. He had slept on his side with his legs toward the front of the truck and his head facing me. I loved traveling with him because I could always reach over and scratch his ear or sit with my hand on his shoulder. On this trip, I swung the armrest in the middle seat up so he could lay his head on my lap. Not a greater feeling in the world.

Naptime was over now, and Moose was eager to get out and explore this new place. I helped him down out of the truck and fastened his leash to his harness. The snow was still falling as he shook it off like dogs do when they are wet, and we proceeded to the front desk. Check-in was uneventful and we went to the elevator with our key in hand. Odie had Isabella, and I had Moose as the doors to the elevator opened, and a fuzzy nose popped out. I don't remember what breed of dog it was, but he was adorable. He was white and a little taller than Moose. They sniffed each other as both puppy parents' faces went from concerned to friendly once we knew neither of our pups was a threat to the other.

We settled into the room as I peered out the window, which overlooked the parking lot. It was dark but still early enough in the evening that people were milling about. I found my truck and noticed how large it was compared to the Audi and other cars around it. Moose immediately jumped on the bed next to the window, and I gave him a pat on the butt. I looked back out the window and noted how beautiful the snow contrasted with the darkness lit up by the orange streetlights. People were passing by my truck and stopping in awe since many of them had never seen a full-size American truck up close. We were in a quaint village far from a military base and would soon depart for the last leg of the journey. Moose slept with Odie and me on a cramped full bed (not a king like we were used to), but I didn't complain. We were safe and together for this move.

I should have been fired from the navigator job because instead of following the main highway through Salzburg like Brad and Katie did, I opted for the shortcut. The path I chose was shorter but carried us up and over the Alps through Innsbruck. It wasn't snowing that morning, but as we started to climb in altitude, the snow started, and it was heavy snowfall. Luckily, the truck and the Audi did fine on traction, but there was a stoppage on one of the highways while the service vehicles were clearing the road. I tried to take a detour but returned to the main road after reading a sign that said in Austrian, "Unless you have chains, do not proceed further." Luckily, the delay wasn't that long, and we were able to reach the other side of the Alps and cross the border into Italy. In hindsight, I don't regret a thing because how many people can say they drove across the Alps in January in a Chevy truck with their dog next to them? Not many, I can tell you that. There's a high likelihood that pride overruled risk management in my decision to take the more dangerous path, but we arrived at Aviano Air Base, Italy, safely on the evening of the second day of travel.

The billeting room was not nearly as comfortable as the lodging in Germany. It was a one-bedroom with a kitchenette and a fold-out couch. We had all our stuff crammed into the living room, and every morning, Chelsey would have to move all her bedding to make a place to sit. Moose seemed to love the close quarters, though. I think he enjoyed having everyone close together and accessible. In Germany, he was separated by the stairs, but here, everyone was around. He mourned the loss of Ginger, but now he was getting all the attention – not just from us but from our other friends as well.

Teresa and Ditty were also in billeting looking for a house so I would text her to let her know when we were taking Moose out for a walk. She would come along with her two sons, Chase and Gabe, but soon, our other friends, "Woody" and Lanissa, would join in with their kids. The kids loved Moose. I knew he wouldn't run, so I would let them take turns being responsible for "walking" him. They would fight over whose turn it was next to hold the leash. He never pulled them, just walked right alongside the rest of us as we passed the fire station and the vet clinic, and arrived at the dog park on base. I would disconnect his leash from his harness and pull a few tennis balls out of my pockets to give to the kids. Moose was on cloud nine. He would retrieve the balls when they threw them and get pats and praise from them. This would go on for about half an hour, and then we would all return to billeting. It was a common routine for the month or so; we lived in billeting while everyone was hunting for a house to live in.

Aviano has no base housing, so when our unit moved to the base the demand went up drastically all at once for rental properties around the area. The nice houses went to the people who moved in November. It was slim pickings for those who waited. You had the option of being in a not-so-nice house close to the base or a nice house more than 30 minutes away. Odie and I agreed that being closer to base was more important since we would only be living in Italy for a year and a half. The trick I pulled in Germany with Irina wasn't going to fly in Italy, so the language barrier was a challenge.

We found a house in the country that had a large yard and a detached garage. My truck was too tall for the garage, so I used it as a workshop. The house was two stories with an apartment set up downstairs which had its own access to an outside door. The upstairs had a kitchen, living room, a bathroom, and two bedrooms. The house came furnished with nice wardrobes since houses in Europe seldom have closets. We sealed the deal and moved in. Our household goods were delivered, and we unpacked some of our stuff, throwing the rest of the boxes in the spare room upstairs.

Moose enjoyed the giant yard. There was a large tree in the front yard, and the entire property was surrounded by a six-foot-high fence with hedges. Access was through a remote-controlled gate that rolled sideways, allowing a vehicle to enter. The street we lived on was dangerous so having the fence and gate meant Moose would be safe from the Italian drivers that would speed past the front of our house. A small, three-foot fence that ran parallel to the house in the backyard partitioned off the back quarter acre. Moose would only go back there when I opened the gate and mowed. There was a cherry tree in the back partition as well, so I wouldn't let him back there unsupervised for fear he would east a poisoned cherry pit. We mostly hung out in the front yard, where the large front porch provided shade and protection from rain. We settled into the hustle and bustle of Italian life, but something was missing.

Chelsey was mourning Ginger, but it had been several months since she passed, and we were in an exciting new place. Chelsey started talking about getting a puppy. I was adamantly opposed to the idea at first because of the fiasco of traveling with pets. I did, however, understand her need for a companion, and Moose would enjoy having a puppy companion around as well. Besides, who doesn't love the excitement of getting a new puppy? The roads were rife with billboards advertising "Pastore Tedesco" puppies. Yes, that translates to German Shephard. She wanted a freaking hyper-ass and potentially aggressive breed that has been striking fear in citizens since World War II. Great!

Reluctantly, I agreed to the new adoption. Odie and I didn't tell Chelsey about it when we set out in the evening under the auspices of "going to try out a new pizza place." The breeder was way out in the country and didn't speak a lick of English. When we pulled up, Chelsey reacted in a logical manner based on her perception of the situation. "Where the heck is the pizza place?" As we got out of the car, the lady met us and led us to a pen where she had two puppies left. There was a small one, obviously the runt, who was so friendly and came running up to the fence. Then there was the big one who, upon seeing us, bolted back into the barn, wanting to have nothing to do with these strange visitors. Teary-eyed, Chelsey pointed to the larger one as the lady retrieved it and brought it over. It was a female, and when Chelsey held her for the first time, I knew I had no choice. We went into the house to finish the paperwork, and I counted out 350 Euros to buy Mariposa and bring her home.

In retrospect, I think it would have been fine to take Moose with us, but we were unsure of the situation, so we left him at home. He was waiting by the door when we pulled up with Mariposa. We placed her on the floor, and she ran into the corner, whining and crying. Moose went over to her and sniffed her as the poor little thing cowered and shook. She was terrified. It took a few days before she started to warm up, but soon, she was comfortable with all of us. Moose and Mariposa were becoming good friends, but we started to see Mari was a bit of a bully. She was more vocal, too. She would bark at Moose if he had a toy she wanted, and when visiting Mia and Nike, she would terrorize poor Nike, who was the sweetest pup.

Early signs of aggression were setting in, and we had to do something about it. We decided to take her to puppy class on base. It was run by the vet on base, who was an incorrigible and stubborn person. As we were trying to put Mari on the insurance, we had to get an initial bill of health. This vet recorded that she had hip dysplasia as a puppy. I threw the B.S. flag and took Mari to a U.S. expatriate who had moved from New York to Italy to set up a practice. His thick accent was hilarious as he said, "There is nothing wrong with this animal." I shredded the paperwork from the base vet.

The puppy class did not go well. There were other German Shepherds among the twenty or so puppies who were playing with each other, painting a picture of overwhelming cuteness. Mari, however, was highly timid and would not leave our side. When she finally did muster the courage to join the pack, she was tackled by another pup and ran to get away. She bumped into a folding table that was leaning against the wall, and it fell with a thunderous crash. That sealed the deal. Mari would never be the same around other dogs again, with few exceptions.

I know this book is about Moose, and, who knows, maybe I'll write one about Mariposa at some point. Lord knows there is enough material, but I feel Mari's story is so intimately intertwined with Moose's that it would be a disservice to omit her tale. Moose and Mari luckily never fought and got along swimmingly. I would come home from work, and they would hear the gate open as I pulled into the driveway. I would get out as Odie would open the front door and release them both to come running and greet me. They did everything together.

*Hanging out with Mariposa on the front porch in Italy*

When the weather got warmer, we would often hang out in the front yard. They would get the zoomies and race around the large tree out front with their ears laid back, streaking like bullets. Fetch was still a thing but needed adjustments to the methods. Mari would grab the ball and not give it back as Moose would sit there watching her as if to say, "This isn't how this game works you dummy." I would grab three balls and rotate them out. I would throw one, and Mari would leave the one she was guarding to run after the thrown ball with Moose. If Moose got it, he would bring it back. If Mari got it, I would throw the second one for Moose and grab the one Mari had left behind. This cycle would repeat itself until they would grow tired, and we would return inside to eat dinner or watch TV.

I mentioned that Moose would never go in the backyard unless I let him, but Mari was either too dense or too stubborn to recognize unwritten rules. She soon grew big enough to leap over the short fence and terrorize the neighbors. They were an older couple whose son and granddaughter lived with them. I never had a problem with the older man, who was actually quite kind, but the son would always yell at me, referring to Mari as "aggressivo." I was apologetic at first, but after a while, I would dismiss him and tell him to kick rocks. The fence was high, and she only got out once when I forgot to shut the gate. I was in the kitchen, and I saw a streak pass by the window, followed by Mari barking. I rushed outside and hollered for her. She had chased a passerby down the adjacent driveway but returned pleased that she had mitigated the "threat." Moose just sat by, watching the chaos as it unfolded. He never left the yard.

As fall set in, we discovered that we had another visitor on the property. It was dusk, and I let the pups out to do their business. I heard Mari yipping, but it was different from when she would bark at the neighbors. I knew they were in the backyard, so I called for them. Mari came streaking around the corner of the house, and Moose followed with a slow meander. As he climbed the steps, I noticed he had something in his mouth. I told him to spit it out, fearing what it might be. It was a baby hedgehog. His gentle nature knew Mari was a threat to the little guy, and he had gently carried it to the house on a rescue mission. I picked it up and we took pictures of him as I released him back into the yard. A few days later, as I was mowing, I discovered that Mari had killed the poor little guy. This short anecdote paints the contrasting picture between Moose and Mari.

We traveled a lot after we discovered the convenience of AirBnB. One weekend, we planned a trip to Croatia since Chelsey had a friend visiting. We took the Audi with the two pups in the back. As we crossed the border to Croatia, I told the guard in Croatian that we were Americans who lived in Italy and wanted to visit "Hrvatska," the Croatian word for their country. He asked for the dogs' pet passports. I turned to Odie, and she looked at me sheepishly. We had left them at the house. I asked the guy at the gate what we could do, and he said with a stoic face, "Leave them here." After a long pause, he cracked a smile and told us to proceed. I'm sure he thought it was hilarious to mess with an American-speaking broken Croatian, but I wasn't amused. I chalked it up as a minor bump in the road and proceeded on our trip.

*Road trip in the Audi*

The Audi was a diesel, and I had to stop for gas along the way. I pumped the gas and paid without thinking anything of it until we got about five miles down the highway. The Audi started sputtering and stopped altogether. It wouldn't start. Odie looked at me and said, "Did you put gas in it?" That's when my heart sank. See, I don't make those mistakes! But I did. I popped the gas cap and smelled the tank. Sure enough, I filled the Audi with gasoline. In my defense, the diesel pumps in the states are green, but in Europe, the gasoline pumps are green. We were stranded. I called Brad, and he came to rescue us. He patiently waited around as the tow truck arrived and transported me and the Audi back to the local mechanic's shop. They drained the tank, but that car never drove the same again.

Not all the trips ended in disaster, though. Our trip to Switzerland was an awesome experience. We rented an apartment attached to a house whose owners shared the fenced yard with the apartment. I didn't know this until I let Mari out, and she scared the hell out of the owner. We kept her leashed for the rest of the trip, but Moose was free to roam as always. This apartment was two stories, and once again, we encountered Moose's kryptonite personified in the European stairs. I got quite the workout on that trip.

While we were in the small town of Sargans, Switzerland, we decided to visit Liechtenstein. Valdez is a beautiful town, and the pups were well-behaved. The town square had quaint restaurants with outdoor seating and little shops to buy trinkets. One of the shops offered to stamp passports for a nominal fee. We had visited multiple countries, but the European Union has an open border policy, so we had never had our passports stamped unless we were flying. We paid the fee to get our stamp and stamped the dogs' pet passports since we remembered to bring them this time. In front of the museum, they had one of those billboards that depicted a mother and father with two children in traditional attire. The faces had holes cut out where you could put your own face for a photo opportunity. Odie and I thought it would be hilarious to put the dogs faces in the kids' holes while Chelsey took a picture of the four of us. There was a group of Asian people nearby who agreed with us and cackled as we were struggling to lift Moose and Mari while still trying to put our faces in the holes. One German tourist even whipped out his fancy camera and snapped a picture of us, which is depicted in the picture that Chelsey took.

*Posing for the tourists in Liechtenstein*

On Thanksgiving weekend, we planned another trip to see Vienna and Bratislava since they are only about fifty miles apart. We took the pups on a train to Bratislava to see the Christmas markets. I found a place to sit with the dogs while Odie and Chelsey did their shopping. Moose was a champ as always, but Mari would lose her coco puffs every time a dog walked by. It was so bad that one of the locals approached me and started screaming in my face. I don't understand angry Slovakians, but I got the distinct impression that we were not welcome. I nodded politely and started making my way to a less dense area, frustrated that Odie and Chelsey were taking so long. The trip concluded without an international incident, but we were starting to realize we were in this for the long haul with Mariposa.

Our tour of Europe was drawing to a close, and it came time to move again. Our son, Kyle, happened to be stationed at Kadena Air Base, Japan, on the island of Okinawa. Odie and I decided it would be a blessing to be stationed with Kyle, Caroline, and Karmine. It was a long shot for a person in my career field to go from Germany to Italy and then to Japan, but I brought it up with my boss with the caveat that I understood the needs of the Air Force outweighed my desires. "Cowboy" was my commander's boss, but I worked directly for him as his executive officer. Cowboy's reply to me (edited, of course) was, "Screw that Ivan! (my callsign) You should get what you want, and the Air Force should give it to you!" My commander and good friend, "Snooch," made some phone calls and presented my case to the functional manager. Ironically, I was on leave in Kadena visiting Kyle when I found out we would be moving in the summer of 2018 from Italy to Japan with two large dogs and a cat. I kept this tactical problem in the back of my mind because I knew we would eventually be moving back to the States, but Japan was a game-changer.

Chelsey decided to move back to the States since she had a love interest in John, now her husband. So, I started working on the logistics of transportation across Asia to Japan for two humans and three fur babies. This wasn't my first rodeo, so I knew pet-friendly billeting was the first step. I booked it six months out. The rotator didn't fly out of Venice at the time, so I started to work on the commercial travel tickets. The cost was about the same as our move to Germany, but we would need to route through Paris before proceeding to Tokyo. The itinerary was ground transportation from Aviano to Venice, Venice to Paris, Paris to Tokyo, and Tokyo to Okinawa. Moose was about to visit his third continent.

# CHAPTER 4:

# ADVENTURES IN JAPAN

The trip to Okinawa started smoothly but would turn out to be the third most stressful day of my life. We were in temporary pet lodging at Aviano Air Base and had a waiver for the third pet since the policy was only two pets per family. I coordinated a local transportation service to take all our bags and the kennels to the Venice Airport. We arrived early and had to wait to even begin checking in. Once we were checked in, we said goodbye to our furry companions as they were carted off to be put on the plane. I made sure that my phone number was on each kennel. Odie and I checked our bags and proceeded to the gate to board. As we took off towards Paris, I could hear Mariposa barking. Everything was going as planned, but Paris would prove to be a challenge.

When we arrived in Paris, we had to go to baggage claim to get our luggage and the pets since the airline wouldn't check our bags through on the international flight to Japan. That meant we had to check them back in once we found the international terminal. We had shipped some items already, but we were traveling with four suitcases and three kennels. When we got to the baggage claim, the bags came out first, and then the pets. They loaded our pups on the baggage carousel, and the kennels came up the conveyor belt and slid down with a crash. Luckily, the pets were okay, and the kennels were undamaged. Odie and I each got two carts, loaded up the kennels and bags on the carts, and proceeded to the international terminal to check in.

On the way, we were struggling horribly. The carts had a lever you had to hold, and if you let go, it would set the brake. I was pushing the cart with Moose and Isabella and a luggage cart. Isabella's kennel was on top of Moose's as I lost control of the luggage cart. When I let go of the cart holding the kennels, the cart came to an abrupt stop and the kennels slid off with a huge crash right in the middle of where the passengers were walking. Not a single person stopped to help us. They just walked around the kennels as I picked them up and made sure Moose and Isabella were still doing well.

We found where we were supposed to go but we had to go up an elevator. The elevator was only big enough for one cart, and there were only two of us. I found an airport employee and asked if I could leave the cart at the top of the floor as I went down to get the other carts that Odie was watching. Of course, the initial response was no, but I explained the predicament, and the person agreed that there was no other way. It took about ten minutes before Odie and I were together with the four carts. We checked in the pets and our luggage once again and made it to the gate in plenty of time. The next big hurdle was over, and we were on our way to Tokyo.

Odie and I had both been to Japan, so we weren't completely taken by surprise when we landed in Tokyo. The experience with the pets in Tokyo was much better than what we experienced in Paris. The staff at the terminal met us as we disembarked the aircraft and ushered us to where our babies' kennels were organized and covered with cargo netting. They were very polite as we went through the paperwork, and they scanned their chips to ensure we weren't smuggling any unregistered animals. After the import paperwork was complete, the staff even transported our pets to our connecting flight and told me exactly where to go to pay the 100 dollars each for the connecting flight to Okinawa. By this time, I was exhausted, so it was very reassuring to have the Japanese employees help so much. Two legs were done, and we were on our final leg to Okinawa.

My good friend Cece was my sponsor for our move to Japan. The Air Force has what is called a sponsor program that assigns incoming families someone to coordinate lodging, pick them up from the airport, and show them around. Stateside moves usually aren't a big deal, but overseas assignments need the program. She brought along our friend Bill as well because Kyle's little car could only transport Odie and me. We had a lot of cargo to carry. I remember landing and walking out to the same baggage claim area I had been when visiting Kyle a few months prior. Our pets were already there and loaded on carts. God bless the Japanese people. Kyle and Caroline helped us with our luggage after we gave Karmine some huge hugs, and we headed out the doors.

Bill and Cece were waiting in their cars. The weather was so hot and humid that day that we began sweating as soon as we left the building. I gave Cece a hug, and Bill came over for his hug. He's about a foot taller than me, and he picked me up in a bear hug. Then he handed me a delicious Japanese alcoholic beverage, told me it was a tradition, and demanded I chug it. Naturally, I obliged. Bill is also a huge dog lover and knew Moose had to go to the bathroom while we were getting everything situated. He couldn't get the zip ties off the kennel door, so he bent the rod that kept the door closed just enough to let Moose out. He apologized for damaging the kennel, but I told him not to worry about it one bit. I couldn't be mad at my friend who just handed me a drink and wanted to take care of my dog! Besides, we were finally here and had a small army to help us out.

The ride to base was about thirty minutes. The first stop was Karing Kennels on Kadena Air Base. I made reservations in advance as soon as we knew our itinerary. There is a six-month quarantine rule in Japan, but the Japanese don't really enforce it on the base. We started the quarantine in Italy, so we only had a few weeks on it when we arrived. The rule was you must keep them away from other animals which we did. We checked them into the kennel and went to our billeting room to drop off the kennels and luggage. Cece and another friend, Rob, had stocked our room with drinks and snacks. Cece also had my nametag for my uniform with my name in English and Kanji letters. We ended up not using the billeting room for anything other than storage since we stayed with Kyle and Caroline until we found a house.

The housing office at Kadena is crazy. Okinawa has multiple bases that house all the branches of the service, but Kadena is the hub. We were not given the option to live off base, which was fine with Odie and me; we wanted to be on base with Kyle and we didn't want to bother with finding a rental on the economy to house three pets. They gave us two options for a house, and both were three-bedroom, two-story quadplexes. The first one we looked at was nice, but the neighbor had a yippy little dog that I knew would be a problem for Mariposa. The second one had a backyard that butted up against a basketball court and a playground. Score! That's the one we picked, but we couldn't move in for a week or so.

Kyle and Caroline had plans to go back to the States a few days after we arrived on the island, so we watched the house for them and took care of their dog, Lily. The great thing about Karing Kennels was that we could sign out the pups to come to visit while they were boarded. Odie and I called it breaking them out of jail, and we signed them out almost every day while we were waiting to move into the house. We tried to get Mariposa and Lily to get along, but it just wasn't going to happen. Moose, on the other hand, got along great with Lily and never had any problems with her the whole time we were at Kadena.

We bought two used cars from the dealership right off base. Both came with an interest-free loan and a two-year warranty. The first was a huge van for transporting cargo like lumber (one of my hobbies is woodworking) and pets. The second was a tiny 3-cylinder, 4-passenger car that I used as my daily driver to and from work. I couldn't get my truck shipped to Japan so these two vehicles would have to do. They ended up working out great for us the entire time we stayed in Japan.

A few weeks after arriving, we moved into the house. It was the second module from the left and was very small in comparison to our two previous houses. It was two stories, but they weren't European stairs, so Moose could easily use them. It was a great neighborhood. Our little section had a total of 12 units in three buildings arranged in a "U" shape. Everyone got along, and we are still friends to this day. They loved Moose, but Mari was a bit much. She would bark at everyone who came near the house or in it. The only exceptions were Kyle, Caroline, and Karmine. I guess she warmed up to them on the ride to base and understood that they were family and part of the pack.

The only issue we had with the house was that there was no fence. This meant that we had to leash up Mariposa and Moose every time they had to go do their business. We needed a fence. Chain-link fence is very expensive for some reason in Japan, but I found a person who was selling some chain links and some posts. I had to get permission from civil engineering who came out and sprayed for electrical lines before I could dig. I did all the work myself and used every inch of the fifty-foot length of chain link. Fifty feet doesn't get you much, though. The width of the fenced-in portion was only about fifteen feet and it only extended to 20 feet from the back of the house. It worked for us, though. We had a place where Mari and Moose could go without being leashed. Mari would lose it when the adorable toy poodle that lived two doors down would occasionally get out. We also worked out an agreement with the neighbors, Emily and Scott, who owned a pit mix named Bailey. I would text them to see if they were outside before letting Mari out. They were great neighbors and very understanding of the situation with Mariposa.

Emily said this about Moose after he passed: "Moose was our neighbor in Okinawa, Japan, and the sweetest boy. We loved seeing him play with his sister, crazy-pants Mari. Being blessed by great neighbors was the highlight of our time in Japan, and was made even better by having Moose next door. Some angels chose fur over wings, and now, sweet boy, you have both."

Dan and Dana were our neighbors on the other side. They had been stationed with me at Tinker, but I didn't know them that well. Dan would drink scotch on his back patio and just laugh when I let the pups out. We would talk about work and the shenanigans that happened on the base. Their little girl Emma was afraid of Mari but loved Moose. All the kids in the neighborhood loved him.

The kids especially liked it when I would let Moose outside the fence. There was an area around the basketball courts that the base kept mowed. It was perfect for fetch, so I would let the neighborhood kids play with him. This was usually when we would have to put Mari away while Kyle was visiting with Lily. Moose could be around them both, but they couldn't be around each other. Moose loved to run free. I would wait until Odie took Mari to bed on the weekends when I would stay up late playing video games. Moose and I would sneak outside, and I would open the gate. He would take off like a shot out of a gun and run through the field. It was usually after midnight, so I didn't have to worry about anyone being out except for once. One night, a couple was taking a very late stroll with their dogs, and Moose ran right up to them. Luckily, the couple's dogs were friendly, and nothing came of it. I ran up and grabbed Moose by the collar, apologizing before realizing that the man was a co-worker named Josh, with whom I had flown numerous times.

We spent a lot of time with the pups in Okinawa, and one of the driving factors was COVID. Japan doesn't do the Airbnb thing, so finding pet-friendly hotels is a little difficult. Plus, there is only so far you can go on an island. Odie and I had plans to travel all over Australia, Vietnam, South Korea, Thailand, you name it. Our plan was to take advantage of spending time with Kyle's family and travel once he moved back to the States. COVID destroyed that plan. Kyle got off the island with his family literally one week before COVID-19 caused the stop-movement order. There were people who had moved out of their house and were told they were not moving. It was a mess, but one good thing that came out of it was spending a lot of time at home with the dogs. We adopted a schedule of taking them for walks, and I spent a lot of time at home. Although we were unable to travel, spending time with the pups was a silver lining.

*All dressed up for a walk in Kadena Air Base, Okinawa, Japan*

We were able to take a few overnight trips on the island, which was fun. The Air Force ran a campsite on the beach in the northern portion of Okinawa, but they had a size limit on the dogs that you could have. Moose and Mari exceeded the fifty-pound size limit, so when we stayed in their cabins, Moose and Mari would stay at Karing Kennel. The Navy, however, ran a campsite on the southeastern side of the island and rented cabins with no size restriction for dogs. That was a fun trip and the time when we discovered Mariposa could swim and actually enjoyed swimming.

The beach was on the eastern portion of the island, and when we took the dogs, the tide was low enough that we could wade to a nearby smaller island. Moose and Mari loved it. I waded out with Mari, and Odie handled Moose. Once we got to the island, I asked Odie if we should let Mari off-leash. She was reluctant at first, but I sarcastically waved my hand and said, "There's no one around, and where's she gonna go? We are on an island." I had a sound argument, so we let them both off-leash as we explored the island for an hour or so. They were fascinated by these sea creatures who would burrow in the sand and feel around with their long tentacles. The tide started to come back, and Odie wasn't a strong swimmer, so I took both dogs when we decided to head back to the mainland. The water that had been knee-deep was now chest-deep, so the pups couldn't wade. They had to swim. Their harnesses had handles that I grabbed and made sure they could stay afloat. I was a little nervous, but they were having the time of their life. We all made it back to shore safely and slept well that night after our adventure at sea.

Our time in Okinawa was coming to an end, and it was time to move back to the States. Our next destination would be a one-year tour at Maxwell Air Force Base in Alabama, where I was lucky enough to be selected to earn a master's degree at the cost of the government. We began preparations for the move. The rotator was our only option this time around because Mari needed a giant-sized kennel instead of the extra-large one we had used before. The commercial flights did not have cargo space for the giant-sized kennel and had a weight limit of 100 pounds. My report date was in the summer, but the rotator only allowed spots for two pets. Odie needed a new car, so we flew out together in April with Isabella under our seat on a commercial flight. The plan was to leave them there with our daughter, Brittany, in Florida, and I would travel back on my own to pack up the house and catch a rotator to the States with Moose and Mari.

The trip went well. We found a car and stayed with Brittany and her husband, Jeff. We spent some quality time with their daughter, Enilia, and received the good news that Brittany was expecting another baby soon. Jeff and I went fishing together and drank a lot of beer before it was time for me to return to Okinawa. COVID restrictions were still in effect, and the government of Japan was enforcing a 14-day quarantine. When I landed in Tokyo, I was ushered to a shuttle that took me to Yokota Air Base on mainland Japan since the Japanese weren't allowing people to catch their connecting flights. I waited there for 13 days before I finally got a space available spot on the rotator going to Kadena. The boredom was excruciating, and I couldn't wait to get back and bail the pups out of prison. I picked them up and took them home as I began the prep for the second most stressful day of my life, the journey with Moose and Mari back stateside.

# CHAPTER 5:
# THE JOURNEY HOME

The second most stressful day in my life came in June of 2021. Odie had gone back to the States ahead of me, and I was left with the task of packing up the house and transporting the two pups, Moose and Mariposa. I disassembled the fence and gave it to a young couple who had just moved to Okinawa. I also handled the movers and packing up the house. Our neighbors, Dan and Dana, watched the house while I was in Yokota for two weeks. When I returned, there was an envelope in which was a voucher for a house cleaning. A very nice gesture on their part saved me a lot of stress. The company guaranteed a passing inspection on the move-out, and we moved into temporary pet lodging.

It was just me with both dogs, so taking them out was usually a fiasco. Many families were also staying in pet lodging, and they were out with their dogs as well. I needed a way to free up both hands to control Mari when she would see other dogs. My solution was a weight-lifting belt with a buckle I could use to attach Moose's leash. A rudimentary solution, yes, but effective. I was able to keep Moose on a leash and control Mariposa as we would wander around the grassy areas to let them do their business. They both slept on the bed with me while we waited around for the day to arrive when we would leave Okinawa.

I secured pet lodging well in advance and returned to Okinawa with a giant kennel in April since the store on base did not carry that size. I was lucky enough to get two spots on the rotator for the dogs, but that wasn't a guarantee. In the week before we were scheduled to leave, word got around on the base of a malfunction with the rotator aircraft. Apparently, someone was shifting luggage around and broke the air conditioner for the cargo space reserved for the animals. People were given the option to go without their pets or stay behind with their pets. I can't imagine the stress those poor people must have experienced.

Our day of departure came, and I was well prepared. The day before departure, I took the dogs to the passenger terminal and weighed them so I wouldn't have to do it the next day. I sold the van to one of our neighbors, and he agreed to let me have it until the day I left. I drove it to the passenger terminal, unloaded my luggage and the dogs, and left the keys in the driver's seat with the van unlocked. Check-in went smoothly, and I ran into a logistician named JD, with whom I worked during an exercise. The objective of that exercise would have failed if JD hadn't been a part of it. We were given the tactical problem of how to refuel two F-15s at Tinian Airfield, which had no jet fuel on the island. Our solution was to fly an R-11 fuel truck on a C-17 cargo plane to the tiny airfield and transfer fuel from the C-17 to the fuel truck and then to the F-15s. The entire movement took less than 24 hours, and JD made it happen, so we had a lot to catch up on.

He helped me with the pups and waited with me in line as we chewed the fat. Once I got the dogs and my bags checked in, I went through the metal detector. I was one of the last passengers to reach the terminal waiting area, and there were no seats available. JD said, "I got you...come with me." He ushered me to the VIP area, where only the high-ranking officers are allowed. There was one family with four kids and plenty of seats. I asked JD, "Are you sure?" His reply was, "Don't worry about it. I run the operations here at this passenger terminal." Sometimes, it's not what you know but who you know. I thanked him and said farewell as I waited to board the rotator.

The call came for all the families to begin boarding. As I made my way to my seat, there were kids crying, cats meowing, and dogs barking. I could hear Mari barking at something and was praying they would be okay. I got settled into my seat, and an employee from the passenger terminal came to my seat. She handed me two laminated cards labeled Moose and Mariposa and informed me that these cards were confirmation that they were loaded and ready to fly. I thought to myself what a good process this was for taking care of people as I fastened my seatbelt and texted Odie that the three of us were boarded. We took off, and our first destination was Yokota Air Base Japan, where we would pick up more passengers.

It's critical to point out that we were traveling toward the end of the COVID pandemic, but it was still a very real threat. People were still wearing masks and on heightened alert. One clearing of your throat would get you a dirty look even though all passengers had to be tested a few days before departure. No one was allowed to travel unless their test came back negative.

We landed at Yokota Air Base on the mainland, and everyone had to deplane so the ground crew could fuel the aircraft for our long trip to Seattle. They also retrieved our pets from the cargo hold. It was a hot day, and the terminal was small. I remember there was a vendor serving the same drink that Bill had given me the day I arrived. It was tempting, but I wanted to keep a clear head.

I made sure I had extra zip ties to fasten to the kennel so I could cut the dogs free if needed. The area for the pets to use the bathroom was not big at all, and there was no way I could maneuver Mariposa in the area without her coming dangerously close to another dog. I let Moose out first and he was totally fine. He did his business and greeted the people and the other pups with sniffs and a wagging tail. Mari was different. I let her out and immediately put her muzzle on. She lunged at the other dogs as I pulled her away from the passenger terminal and behind the bus which was parked on the tarmac close to the taxiway. I was minding my own business when some dude in uniform came and asked me what I was doing. I told him I had an aggressive dog and wanted to protect the other passengers. He told me that I needed to return to the terminal, and I couldn't be out there. I asked him why and he said, "for security."

I had been in the Air Force for over twenty years at this point and never heard a bigger crock of, you know what. I looked at the dude and then at the empty flightline with no airplanes anywhere close and asked him, "security for what? The bus?" Naturally, the dude didn't have an answer and reverted to 2-year-old mode, repeating the same narrative that I was a security risk, and it wasn't safe, blah, blah, blah. That wouldn't be the last time I would encounter this person or his stupidity.

I took my time walking back as I put Mari back in her kennel. I didn't want to leave their side, so I stayed outside with them for most of the time we were waiting. Air Force passenger terminals are nothing like airports, where you have bars, restaurants, places to shop, and things to occupy your time. There was no food other than a vending machine with sandwiches. I did go inside to buy a drink and get the dogs some water, but my stomach was already upset, and I didn't want to risk getting sick on a ten-hour flight. Not everyone applied my method of risk management though. The older teenage boy, who was with his family in the VIP section at Kadena, bought and munched down a chicken salad sandwich, setting in motion a series of butterfly effect events worthy of a time travel movie.

The time came to board the plane once again. They carted the animals to the airplane, and I watched from my window as the kennels were placed into the cargo hold. I settled into my seat, anxious to get back to the States, where Odie was checked into a hotel in

Seattle. We had agreed that we were not going to put our precious pups on any more planes, so we rented a large SUV and planned a road trip from Seattle to Florida with the pups. Some would say that this was a terrible idea, but after being stranded on an island during COVID, where the highest speed limit was 80 kilometers an hour, the thought of being on the open road with a V-8 under the hood was quite appealing.

I texted Odie that we were boarded, but then things started to turn for the worse. I noticed that we had been waiting to taxi for a while. I was about to ask the flight attendant if there was a mechanical failure, fearing the same situation that had occurred a week earlier with the air conditioning system. That was when I saw a paramedic walk by toward the front of the plane. I looked at the guy next to me and our eyes both got wide. Apparently, the teenager who had eaten the sandwich vomited on his way up the airstairs while boarding. The paramedic was checking him out and there seemed to be some disagreement as to his condition for travel. He and the father were saying that he was good to continue, but one of the flight attendants was not comfortable with it.

This debate seemed to last for what seemed like an hour before the father finally made the decision that they would deplane and let the rest of us go. I thought to myself, "about time someone made a decision." As the six passengers left the plane, the rest of us felt sympathetic but wanted to press on. That would not happen as we expected. No, the passengers who disembarked are required under law to retrieve their checked luggage. Now, we aren't talking about a small plane heading to a leisurely location like Cozumel or the Bahamas. We are talking about a large plane filled with people with two to four kids and luggage whose contents are meant to sustain their lives for a few weeks. The family that disembarked had twenty bags between the six of them, and the pilot would not leave until the ground crew could find all their bags.

Time went on for hours while they tried to retrieve these bags. I began to look at my watch. Being a career aviator, I deal with concepts like fuel consumption and crew rest timings daily. After about three hours of delay, I started doing the math. Fuel consumption was probably okay since we hadn't started engines, but the crew duty day could be an issue. We were with the same flight deck crew that flew us from Kadena to Yokota. They have a limited amount of time they can work before going back into crew rest. The specific timings vary based on the situation, but I knew we were cutting it close. I asked the flight attendant how many hours left of their crew day the pilots had left. She said, "enough for now, but not for long."

Well, we ended up passing the point where we could take off and still land in Seattle within the allotted crew duty day. The pilots immediately left the plane and headed to lodging to begin their crew rest. Everyone on the aircraft was told to get off and wait in the terminal. Someone made the genius decision to pull all the bags off the aircraft and line them up. The pups were also unloaded and in a separate area. It was going to be a long day. I was walking around by the dogs when our security friend came over and told me I wasn't allowed to be over there. I asked him why not, and he said something about keeping everyone together. I just rolled my eyes and complied.

By this point, people were getting restless. There were no food services available and not enough seats. Kids were sprawled out on concrete steps with blankets, trying to sleep. Eventually, the base sent some people with frozen sandwiches and potato chips to tide us over. Then, the decision was made to take all the passengers to a billeting room for the night. Then, our security friend told us that we would need to take all our bags and our pets with us. I couldn't believe this insanity. By the time we would get all the luggage loaded in trucks, and people checked into their rooms, they would be three hours from show time. Why not give people the option to stay in the terminal? This guy was stubborn, though, and he had the power. One man confronted him with how stupid his idea was and was met with the threat that if the guy didn't comply, he wouldn't let him board the rotator.

The arrangements of where everyone was supposed to be assigned to stay were chaos. They had people loading up on the wrong trucks, going to the wrong buildings, you name it. Most of the passengers were simply trying to do the right thing, but they loaded Moose and Mari on a truck without talking to anyone. Thank goodness I caught it in time, and I went running up to take them off. The security dork found me behind the line and again confronted me. I went into unfiltered mode. I told him his plan was stupid, it created nothing but chaos, and I nearly lost positive control of my pets because of him. I then told him I was not following his made-up rules anymore and would not leave my dogs unattended because I had zero faith in his competence. Surprisingly enough he backed down and left me alone the rest of the time I was at Yokota. I texted JD since he was in the same career field as my new friend. JD confirmed my opinion of this guy's poor decision-making.

Once the people started trickling out on trucks, I was able to get a solid answer of where I was to go and how I would get there. A truck came to pick up me and the dogs with our luggage and took us to the lodging front desk. It was about two in the morning and after I unloaded our stuff, the truck drove away into the night. I left all the bags and the pups outside as I went to the front desk to get my key. They were very polite as I confirmed I had a pet room. They said yes, but it was on the other side of base. I was visibly shaken up and frustrated when a maintenance man entered the lobby. He asked me if those dogs were mine. I replied yes. Then he offered to give me a ride to the other side of base. I was so relieved. He dropped me off and gave me his phone number. We agreed to meet up at the same place at 0700 the next morning to start the process for a second time.

I got very little sleep in those five hours, but I was at least able to let Moose and Mari out of their kennels and feed and water them. They slept like rocks as I was in and out, trying not to oversleep and miss our plane. The friendly maintenance man came back as he promised, and I left a little cash on his dashboard before I shook his hand and thanked him. I was way early to the passenger terminal but first to go through the line with the dogs. They were well-rested, and I proceeded past the metal detector and into the holding area. It looked different in the morning light and filled me with a sense of hope.

I told Odie about the delay, and she said not to worry. She would just stay in the hotel for an extra day, which would delay our arrival to Florida by a day. We had plenty of time. The passengers slowly started arriving with their luggage and began filling the area. People were sitting wherever they could in anticipation of boarding. One passenger partook a little too much alcohol in the short amount of time between leaving the terminal and returning. He passed out on the ground. The paramedics came to put him on a gurney and take him to the hospital. As they walked by, I said, "He has his luggage, right?" I'm sure he got into some trouble for "missing a movement," as the military calls it, but I wasn't sympathetic at all. He made his choice and I just wanted to make sure it wasn't going to affect anyone else.

Finally, the time came to board. We had a healthy aircraft and a rested crew, and soon, we would be over the Pacific Ocean. My seat was cramped, but I was so grateful for it and the spots for Moose and Mari. Soon, Moose would be back in America, and Mari would be seeing America for the first time. The only delay on this second attempt was caused by the flight attendant missing one person with the headcount.

Everyone began murmuring about how we didn't care. Leave them behind! We were all ready to get out of Yokota. The issue resolved itself when they found the person in a similar condition to the drunk guy. We pressed with two less passengers to Seattle.

I was in and out of sleep the whole flight, dozing off between movies. I would start watching a movie and then become fascinated with what was playing on my neighbor's screen. The flight was long, so I was exhausted when we arrived. As soon as I got off the plane, I asked the nearest person where my pets were. I heard something, something, counter past customs, something, something. I was the first passenger to make it to the baggage claim. Odie was there to meet me. I embraced her and started crying and whispered, "We did it, babe." They brought Mari and Moose, who were excited to see Mom after a few months of being apart. We took them outside and cleaned them up. Moose had pooped in his kennel, so I just trashed the bedding and wiped down the inside of the kennel and Moose. I broke the kennel down with the peace of knowing he would not be placed back in it for the rest of the trip. No, he would sit comfortably in a rented SUV for the remainder of the trip.

We waited and waited for my luggage, and it never came. I decided to ask someone and as I was walking to the nearest counter, my name came over the intercom. "Passenger Ivie, please proceed to customs to receive your luggage and process customs." Apparently, I was in such a hurry to get to the dogs that I completely bypassed customs. They had my two bags there and asked if I was smuggling anything. I told them no, and they released my luggage to me as Odie and I left the airport for the hotel.

We had plans to go to dinner that night with our friends Doug and Liz. I wanted to sleep but needed to reset my circadian rhythms to the time change, so I powered through to meet them for dinner. It was great catching up, but the next day, we would hit the road on a grand adventure through the Northern United States across the Mississippi River and down through the deep south to Florida. The second most stressful day of my life had ended, and we would be on the open road with Moose and Mariposa.

I purchased a seat cover for the rental car, and it helped a little, but Mariposa's German Shepherd hair gets everywhere. It didn't matter, though, because they were happy and content not being cooped up in a kennel underneath a noisy airplane. I purchased them brand new harnesses, and we strapped each harness to the female end of the seat belt in the back seat. We put some small luggage on the floorboards to make a level platform with soft blankets. We broke the kennels down, and they fit nicely in the cargo space toward the rear of the SUV.

We set out on our first day with the goal of getting out of Washington state and well into Montana before bedding down. It was a challenge to be driving on the right side of the road again, but it didn't take long to get back into the swing of things. The dogs were excited to get on the road. Moose laid right down and chilled immediately. Mari took a little longer. She was restless until we got out of Seattle, but then she calmed down. She always knew when we were about to stop for a potty break and would start whining. The first day went well. Odie offered to drive, but I was enjoying myself. The weather was beautiful, and the scenery was picturesque. We drove for over twelve hours before we arrived in Billings, Montana, for the night. Odie and I had dinner, fed the pups, and went straight to bed.

The next day was beautiful. We planned to rise early on the second day because we wanted to see Mount Rushmore before sunset. The drive to Rapid City was about six hours, so if we left by seven o'clock in the morning, we would get there around one or two o'clock. Along the way, I saw signs for the Battle of Little Bighorn. I mentioned to Odie that I always wanted to see Custer's last stand. We were having a good time, so she was cool with me looking around for a little bit. She has little interest in historical sites, so she stayed in the car while Moose napped and Mari barked. I enjoyed walking around and listening to the tour guide. He pitched his book and recommended another in the gift shop. I purchased both books and some refrigerator magnets for Odie before getting back on the road. We arrived at Mount Rushmore around two o'clock. It was quite impressive. The parking garage was covered, and the weather was cool, so we left the dogs in the car with the windows cracked. Odie and I went up to the monument and took pictures, after which I returned to the car while she shopped. We stayed at a nice hotel that night, but the next morning was going to be even earlier.

The next day, we planned to stop at the baseball field in Iowa where the Kevin Costner movie *Field of Dreams* was filmed. I loved that movie since I was a kid and couldn't pass up the opportunity to go see it. The site closed in the early evening, and the drive was over ten hours to Dyersville, Iowa. The only way I could see the house, the cornfields, and the bleachers was to leave at four in the morning. I was still used to Japan time, so it wasn't hard for me, but Odie and the pups showed fatigue. All three of them slept for the first two hours of the drive until the sun came up. I kept glancing over to Odie and then back at Moose and Mari, thinking how fortunate I was to have the opportunity to drive across the country with them.

We arrived at the movie site about an hour before they closed, so I paid my money to get the tour of the house. It was just like it was in the movie. Very little was changed. Odie stayed in the car with the pups while I went on the tour and walked around the field and in the corn. We left the car running for them while we took fifteen minutes in the gift shop. I checked *Field of Dreams* off my bucket list, so we hit the road to our next stop in Bettendorf, Iowa, where we would stay the night. I was nearly falling asleep by the time we pulled up to the hotel, and I deliberately didn't gas up in Bettendorf because we had big plans on our fourth day of travel.

We slept in a little on the fourth day and didn't leave the hotel until about seven in the morning. Our first stop was a place that laid claim to being the biggest truck stop in the world located in Walcott, Iowa. We spend about an hour buying random trinkets, filling up with gas, and getting breakfast. The pups, of course, got some snacks, too, since we were spoiling the heck out of them the whole trip. After we had our fill of the truck stop, we continued the course to Murfreesboro, Tennessee. We arrived in enough time to get the dogs bedded down and have a nice dinner. The next day would be our last leg and the most stressful and worst day of my life. Our lives were about to change forever.

We arose around six in the morning. I was in the bathroom when I heard Odie's phone ring. I heard her screaming our oldest daughter's name over and over, asking Brittany if she was sure. "Brittany! No! Are you sure? No! Brittany!" Something horrible had happened. At first, I thought it might be the kids' biological father, but Odie wouldn't be reacting that way. Then I thought it might be Brittany and Jeff's little girl, Enilia – our oldest granddaughter. I came out of the bathroom and asked what was going on. Odie said goodbye to Brittany and that we were on our way. Then she turned to me and said, "Jeff was killed in a car accident." It took me a few minutes to register and then I was still asking questions like how, when, it's impossible, etc. Once it sank in, I got sick to my stomach. My son-in-law, a Navy Chief Petty Officer and father of our granddaughter with another on the way, was no longer with us on this earth. The date was 17 Jun 2021.

I tried to comfort Odie, but there was little comfort to be had by either of us. We had a task at hand to get to Brittany. We finished up our morning routine, loaded up the dogs, and set out to our last destination, Jacksonville, Florida. By the time we got to Jacksonville, Odie had talked to Brittany multiple times, and we were beginning to put the pieces together. It had been a head-on collision as he was leaving the housing area, literally a stone's throw from their front door. As we drove by, we saw the skid marks and debris from an accident. Odie got out of the car first to give Brittany a hug while I gave them their space and took the dogs to the backyard.

While Brittany was figuring out what to do, Odie and I decided to put the dogs up in a nice kennel near her house. It was a brand-new kennel and even had a swimming pool. We checked them in and returned to Brittany's house. We all agreed that Brittany would need to handle a lot of things before a funeral could even happen, so we took Enilia with us to Oklahoma so Brittany could focus on making the arrangements. I was not due at Maxwell Air Force Base for another month, so we left the dogs in Florida as we made our way to Oklahoma for some leave.

Jeff's loss hit all of us in a profound way. I miss him dearly and see him in the two girls. I can't help but wonder if that kid had not eaten that sandwich, would I have arrived a day earlier? Maybe Jeff and I would have had too many beers the night before he was killed. Then maybe he would have left later for work and not had the accident at all. A person can go crazy thinking through all the possibilities.

The funeral was officiated magnificently by Jeff's commanding officer. Brittany knew she could not live in that house in Florida and decided to sell it in favor of moving to Oklahoma, knowing that there was a high likelihood Odie and I would return to Oklahoma City after I was done with school. We swung by the kennel and broke Moose and Mari out before we drove to Prattville, Alabama, where we would stay for a year. We moved into the house Brad and Katie were living in since Brad had gone to school a year before me. It just worked out that way.

I loved my time in Alabama. Odie was gone a lot, but I understood why. She had to help Brittany move and get settled in Oklahoma. Both of our daughters were pregnant at the same time and had their babies a few months after Jeff's death. Chelsey gave birth to Evalyn in October, and Brittany gave birth to Esker in December. In the span of a few months, our grandchildren doubled.

While Odie was away, I would get the chance to spend a ton of time with the pups. Losing Jeff changed the way I looked at things, and the tempo of being in school slowed my life pace. I would get up in the morning and take the dogs outside while I did my reading in the backyard. I would take a break from time to time and throw the ball for them. Class for the first semester started at 12:30 PM and was over before four o'clock on most days. Plus, the dogs had way more room in the bed with one less human. They were soaking it up. Once I started writing papers, I would hang out with Moose and Mari in the fourth bedroom I converted into an office. Both would curl up on the floor. Moose would doze off while Mariposa always kept a close eye out by peering through the front window.

Life in Alabama was a needed break from the fast pace we had been living for the last six years. I took full advantage of it, but Moose was slowing down. We used the same vet that Brad and Katie used while they were in Alabama. When we took Moose in, he was diagnosed with early stages of osteoarthritis in his hind legs. Additionally, he had a broken tooth that needed extracting. Mari also had a broken tooth. They both had to be put under for the extraction. Mari did well, but Moose had a history of his blood pressure dropping dangerously low while under anesthesia. That was the last time he underwent any procedure because we were afraid to lose him. As a result, his dental health quickly deteriorated over the next few years, and his mobility began to decline.

One day, when I was in the backyard of the Alabama house, I was playing fetch with Moose. I tossed the ball up in the air like I had done a hundred times before. He leaped to catch it in mid-air, and as he jumped, his hips gave out, and he lost his balance, landing hard on the concrete slab. This was when I recognized that although his heart was still strong, his arthritis was beginning to affect his quality of life. That was the last time I played fetch with my buddy because I was too afraid that he would injure himself. He was still able to jump on the couch and he still enjoyed walking around the backyard. He still had a healthy tail wag but needed help getting on the bed. I would have to lift him on the bed at night or when we would take naps. He was still able to jump off the bed, but his mobility was deteriorating.

I finished up school at Maxwell, and once again, the movers came. This time, we had all the stuff we accumulated overseas plus all the stuff we put in long-term storage while we were overseas. The truck was packed so full the driver was strapping things to the back and putting our stuff in the compartments designed for his tools and straps. We watched the truck drive away, knowing our next move would be to Oklahoma. Once again, I had people in key places who understood the context and realized that although not technically a hardship tour, Brittany's situation was as close as you could get to a hardship tour. Moose was returning to the same house he had lived in as a puppy. So once again we hit the road in Odie's new Tahoe as I drove my truck with a rented trailer. She had Isabella, and I had the dogs. It would be Moose's last move.

# CHAPTER 6:

# THE BIG SCARE

# AND DECLINE IN HEALTH

Although we had noticed he was slowing down in Alabama, Moose was still very active when we returned to Oklahoma in the summer of 2022. He could still walk outside and would get excited when we would return home. His tail would wag, and he'd pant happily. There were no signs of impending doom, and he seemed very happy to be living in the same house as before. Odie began Nana's daycare with the two babies, and he seemed to have a youthful demeanor around the children. In July, things changed.

We had noticed that he wouldn't wag his tail as much and seemed to be getting pickier with his food. Odie would cook up what we called the "dog slop," which consisted of rice, chicken, and vegetables that we would mix with his food. Every feeding involved grabbing the food bowls and mixing the slop with their dry food. About the time the slop ran out was usually when Moose would begin to turn his nose up. Odie would counter by adding a new ingredient like hamburger or pumpkin, but he would soon get pickier and pickier.

Moose still loved the scraps, though. Odie would put the two critters in the master bedroom while she fed the babies, Evalyn and Esker. Those two little ones would throw their food on the floor like all babies do. Odie would clean them up, put their clothes back on, change their diapers, and put them in the playroom. This was when the feeding frenzy would begin. Moose and Mari could hear the commotion of cleaning up the babies, which was their cue to assume their role as vacuum cleaners. Odie would open the door, and Mari, being younger and spryer, would always come out first. Moose, however, could still hold his own. He would scarf up the food after Odie would make sure there were no grapes, tomatoes, or other harmful foods for dogs. It got to the point where she would pick up most of the food on the floor, add it to what was left on the highchair trays, and place it in their bowls in equal amounts so Moose would always get his fair share.

Dinner time with Odie and me was always a fun time, too. We have a coffee table with a top that lifts to allow you to eat from the couches in the living room. We always eat our dinner at this table while we watch our TV shows. Mariposa usually kept her distance, while Moose did not. He would wedge himself in between the couches at our feet and get stuck looking for anything we may have dropped. We never fed him directly from the table, but he began to anticipate the sound of the tabletop being lowered. Pavlov would be proud because Moose always associated this sound, like the ringing of a bell, with getting whatever scraps we would have left over. It became a habit of saving just a little bit of steak or chicken for the pups. I cherish the memories of that routine, which continued even after Moose's health started to deteriorate.

In July, they both came due for their annual check-ups, so we found the place that we had used as a kennel when we first arrived. We chose the place based on good reviews and the atmosphere. Mariposa did her standard barking at every four-legged thing in the place as we walked in, and even a few two-legged staff members. Moose was the exact opposite. He was friendly toward all things, four or two-legged. This visit was when we met Dr. "Smith". Mari passed all her tests with flying colors, but Moose had some issues. Dr. Smith noticed his tail wasn't wagging, and he had lost some muscle mass in his hips. He recommended a medication that was new, and we got a few doses to try out, which we hoped would ease the pain in his hips.

I won't name this medication for liability reasons, and I can't prove that the medication caused his symptoms, but I have my suspicions. A few days after taking this medication, he immediately stopped eating and was unable to walk straight. Odie called while I was at work, and I rushed home. On the way, I called Dr. Smith, furious that the medication had presumably caused him to get sick. Dr. Smith was the voice of calmness and told us to stop administering the medication and to bring him in. I brought him in and had to carry him into the clinic. Dr. Smith ran some tests and discovered his blood count was dangerously low. He took multiple blood samples and checked his stool for blood. There was no blood in his stool, so the prognosis was possibly internal bleeding.

Dr. Smith recommended an expensive sonogram procedure at a local emergency clinic costing four figures. I asked him how much exactly, knowing that we had insurance, and, even if we hadn't, I would pay whatever to find out what was wrong with Moose. Dr. Smtih's demeanor changed, and I knew Moose was in trouble. The one ray of hope I had was after Dr. Smith took his blood, Moose ate a small amount of canned food as a treat for being such a good boy. I was still in uniform and left in such a hurry that I didn't even settle the bill.

I hurried to the 24-hour clinic after Dr. Smith called ahead to let them know I was on my way. They had me sign some documents, including the expected cost of the procedure. On the counter was a candle with a sign that said, "If this candle is burning, please be quiet out of respect for someone who is saying goodbye." They took Moose back, and I waited in a small, sterile room with pictures of pets on the walls and advertisements for flea and tick prevention. It seemed like an eternity until a young lady walked in and introduced herself. She said that the procedure went well, and Moose's blood count was much higher than what Dr. Smith had reported. I immediately broke down, relieved, and was embarrassed since I was still wearing my uniform. She went on to explain the findings. We weren't out of the woods yet.

Apparently, there is a very aggressive form of cancer that large dogs often encounter. It grows on blood-rich organs like the spleen, heart, or lungs. It is especially dangerous because, when found, it is often too late. The tumor ruptures, causing internal bleeding, and unless caught quickly, death comes within hours. The treatment usually involves surgery to remove the tumor and follow-on chemo sessions. Moose's prognosis, however, baffled the doctor. She explained that she didn't see any tumors on his vital organs. His heart and lungs were healthy, and she could not explain what would cause the internal bleeding. This is where it got weird. She said she saw a mysterious growth throughout his body cavity that resembled spider webbing. I was devastated. I asked her if surgery or chemo was an option, to which her reply was a no in a soft voice. She said they could attempt to gather a biopsy from him and determine what the strange webbing was, but it was a risk to put him under since his heart rate dropped to a dangerous level the last time he was put under in Alabama for a broken tooth. She added that the samples were often unsuccessful because it is difficult to align the probe and gather the sample, especially in Moose's case. I reasoned that since it wouldn't change anything, doing nothing was the best course of action. She then said I could take Moose home and told me to monitor him closely. Her final words to me were, "Take care of him, but begin considering his quality of life."

The aides brought Moose back out to me, and he was walking on his own. They gave us some herbal medication called Yunnan Baiao, which helps blood clot properly without becoming too thin. It was not a prescription medication, so it was not covered under our insurance policy, but it didn't matter.

I put him back in the truck, and we started home. When we arrived, Moose seemed to be in much better spirits, and I explained the whole thing to Odie. We were confused because we weren't sure he had cancer, but we weren't sure he didn't. This was when we started research on cancer-preventative herbs to add to his diet.

I reached out to my brother-in-law, Carlos, whose dachshund had recently passed from skin cancer. Peanut had a good quality of life during his bout with cancer, and I wanted to know what Carlos had done to help him along. He sent me a few links to some things that he used, one of which was dandelion root, which could be roasted and boiled down as an additive to the dog's water. The best piece of advice he gave was to stay positive. He told me that the worst thing I could do was to act mopey and sad. I think I already knew this, but it was good to hear it from him as a reminder to keep a positive attitude.

Odie started researching things and added hemp seed, organic honey, apricots, blueberries, and raspberries into Moose's diet for their cancer-fighting qualities. We also added turmeric to the list since it is known for preventing symptoms of arthritis. Odie began buying alkaline water to add to the dandelion root as well. We knew that nothing was for sure, but anything we could do couldn't hurt. This marked the beginning of how our lives would change for the next year and a half. Previously, feeding was simply scooping dry food and mixing it with the wet concoction Odie would cook on a weekly basis. Now, feeding time was a huge ordeal. It involved chopping apricots, defrosting blueberries in the microwave, adding honey, and mixing in his medications. We even began using a pill box to track his medication.

At this point, he was on Gabapentin, which Dr. Smith had prescribed after the other medication presumably made him sick, thyroid medicine, and Yunnan Baiao. The prescription meds were easy to find, but the Yunnan Baiao proved to be difficult at first. Dr. Smith could not order it. I tried a 24-hour clinic, but they were low and would not give me any. I went to the major pet stores to ask if they carried it, and of course, they didn't. I was about to give up when a clerk from the pet store recommended the Asian market. Odie and I traveled downtown to the Asian market and scoured the shelves to no avail. Then Odie pointed out a counter toward the front. I approached the elderly man there, asked if they carried it and showed him a picture. He said they did, but it was in a powder form. He then asked why I needed it, and I explained it was for Moose. He said that made sense since many horse owners from the local racing track would use it for their animals. We bought two vials of the herbal preventative and ended up using it only for emergencies since I later found an online source for it.

After a few days, Moose miraculously returned to his old self. The Gabapentin did wonders for his pain, and he was galloping around the backyard, wagging his tail and playing with Mariposa. I took him in for a check-up, and Dr. Smith was amazed at how the muscles in his hips had been restored. He remarked that Moose was a "champ" and how rare it was to see a dog make a recovery so late in life. Moose was thirteen and a half at the time. His mobility was great but also to a fault. He would bite off more than he could chew sometimes or push himself too hard and get sore when the medication would wear off. He could still climb the stairs, but getting back down was a challenge. My dad is an old cowboy, and he said that horses always do better going uphill and struggle going downhill. Dogs have similar anatomy. One day, Moose came bounding down the stairs, took a bad tumble on the tile floor, and slammed into the wall. I gasped and went to pick him up, thinking that he had injured himself. Luckily, he was fine, but we began closing the door to the laundry room that led to the stairs. That was the last time Moose would hang out with me upstairs. Eventually, I set up the spare bedroom with my gaming systems so the pups could hang out.

I'll break here from the narrative to explain my experiences with dogs sleeping on the bed. Debates abound on whether a dog should get on the furniture or not, and at first, I was adamantly opposed. Moose changed my attitude. He slept in between Odie and me every night and always enjoyed naps with Mom. There were times when I would deliberately be late for work because Moose would have his head lying on my stomach. There was no way in hell I was going to move and get out of bed, spoiling those precious moments. I remember one night after I had a bad day at work when my commander and I didn't see eye to eye on how we were executing an upcoming alert inspection. For the record, our squadron crushed the inspection and pulled out the first mission-ready rating the wing had achieved in five years after a failed evaluation. But at the time, I felt very defeated. I went to bed like always, knowing the crew was showing up for a step brief the next morning. My head was racing with flashbacks to my conversation with the commander and all the things that could go wrong. Then Moose shifted in bed and laid his body lengthwise next to mine. I could feel his warmth and the soft rhythm of his breathing. It was the best night's sleep ever. Dogs have a calming sense about them, and Moose knew his dad needed calming. So, for anyone out there who says dogs shouldn't sleep on the bed, I'm here to tell you that you are dead wrong...hands down.

Moose always slept well and, thankfully, continued to sleep well. I still had to lift him up on the bed, but occasionally, he would jump off when he wasn't supposed to. He could still jump up on the couch as well, and this continued for a while until February, when things took a turn for the worst. I again received a phone call from Odie saying something was wrong with my little buddy. She said he couldn't walk without falling, his head was cocked to the side and moving erratically, and his eyes were shifting back and forth and occasionally rolling to the back of his head. I rushed home immediately. When I arrived, he was on the bed, showing the symptoms Odie had explained. I told her, "This isn't good," fearing that a tumor in his brain may have appeared.

I packed Moose up and rushed him to the 24-hour emergency clinic we had been to before. They brought out a gurney for him and took him inside for an examination. I waited in the same room as before, and the doctor came in. My voice cracked when I asked, "What is wrong with him?" She simply said, "This dog is dizzy and experiencing anxiety from the dizziness." I asked if it was a brain tumor, to which she replied, "No." Then, she went on to explain that he was experiencing a disease known as idiopathic vestibular disease. No one knows why it happens, but it is quite common in older dogs. The symptoms are extreme dizziness and wobbly motions when walking. The cause is that the vestibular nerve that connects the ear to the brain ceases to function properly. She told me the first 72 – 96 hours are the worst, and it typically gets better over time. She prescribed some very expensive medication and sent us home, explaining that he should avoid slippery floors and would need to be held up when using the bathroom or eating.

We took Moose home, and he seemed to calm down a little bit. We set up the kennel for him for the first time in years because we had to limit his movements. He was defecating and urinating on himself in the kennel because he couldn't stand up. The third night was exceptionally bad, and Odie and I thought it was over and decided to take him in to be euthanized. We had him in the kennel with the top off and brought him into the living room. We brought out Isabella to say goodbye, and this is when the crazy dog blew our minds. Isabella let out a meow, and Moose popped his head up like nothing happened. It was temporary, but we knew he was still fighting, and we would help him fight. I learned over the course of the next two weeks that when he would start getting dizzy and anxious, the only remedy was to lay him on the bed and lie on top of him with my body to calm him down. Eventually, he was able to move around thanks to a way less expensive steroid that Dr. Smith prescribed for him. Once again, "Miracle Moose," as we began calling him, had beaten Mother Nature's call for death.

In the months following his onset of vestibular disease, we took every opportunity to take him places and build more memories. There are two trips that serve as my fondest memories while he was sick. He loved car rides, so whenever we planned a trip, I would try to find lakefront properties to rent since I liked to fish, and the dogs loved to be around nature. It was always a concern that they would make a mess or tear up something, but I realized that most owners who allow pets at their properties understand being a dog owner. I always kept honest communication with the owners and made sure the yard was cleaned before we left. Odie has always been very thoughtful about housekeeping wherever we go, as well.

The first trip we took was to Lake Jackson on Memorial Day in May of 2023 for my nephew's graduation. Moose was still getting around well and enjoyed the setup. It was a nice house right on Lake Brazoria, and the backyard was huge, with plenty of room for them to explore and sniff new things. This location was especially suited for our needs because the terrain wasn't too steep, and there were no steps. I had the opportunity to take the dogs out and let them run while I went out the back gate on the dock and fished. Didn't catch a thing that weekend. The owners had set up a garage with insulation, a couch, a big-screen TV, a ping pong table, a foosball table, and an air hockey table. Karmine and I were in heaven. They also placed two sets of bunk beds in the far area, and there was a bathroom. "Us mens," as Karmine would say, stayed in the garage with Moose and Mariposa, just hanging out. The best part was the flooring, which was an epoxy garage coat and highly resistant to any liquids. We felt very comfortable leaving the pups in the climate-controlled area when we were gone because any messes would be a quick kill to clean up. And wouldn't you know it? Moose didn't have a single accident the whole weekend!

The second trip I remember was about two hours east of Oklahoma City at a cabin in a small town named Canadian near Lake Eufaula. This time, it was Labor Day weekend. The place wasn't as luxurious as the one in Lake Jackson, but the fishing was way better. I caught several fish that weekend, and the pups seemed to really like the trees and the wildlife. I found a tiny land tortoise the size of a quarter that trip, which the pups were both very curious about. Moose had a hard time with the terrain since it was very steep, leading out to the back gate, which led to the dock. He stumbled and fell a few times but was able to get up and press on. Another downside was the back porch had steps leading down to the yard. I would have to carry Moose every time we went out. We had no big plans this weekend, though, and it was just the four of us, so it wasn't a big inconvenience. Odie suggested this trip when I wanted to save money, but I am glad we went. It was relaxing, and we built some good memories with Moose, except for the mess he made on the comforter that I had to pay the owners for. It was totally worth it, though. This was the last trip we would take with Moose.

*His last trip to the cabin at the lake*
*(notice his head tilt)*

# CHAPTER 7:

## SAYING GOODBYE

Moose was never quite the same after his bout with vestibular disease. Coupled with his osteoarthritis, it became difficult for him to do simple tasks like eating and doing his business. The final two weeks were the worst, which is to be expected, with an animal's final moments. I would need to help him outside and hold him up to keep him from collapsing. At times, I would let him go, and he would fall, which was heartbreaking, especially a few times when he would take a nosedive, and you could hear his fragile body hit the ground. He would also lose control of his bowels quite frequently. My wife and I would dread leaving the house because we never knew what we would come back to. We ordered special blankets for the bed that would prevent any fluids from seeping through, but our lives consisted of constantly washing blankets, washing towels, scrubbing carpets and rugs, and, the worst...cleaning Moose. I would wake up three to four times a night just to avoid the cleaning, but he made messes more often than he didn't. Through it all, not once did we ever get upset with him.

Granted, we despised the situation, but every day was precious. Up until this point, my wife and I were in agreement that it was not time. Being a stay-at-home puppy mom, Odie had a different perspective than I did. The Friday before Thanksgiving, I came home from work after talking to our vet, who had mentioned a shot for arthritis that he said drastically increases the quality of life in pups with arthritis problems. Moose had experienced an exceptionally bad day. It was then that she suggested that it might be time. I was not ready to admit that the time had come, so I resisted and made him an appointment to get the shot on Monday. I had high hopes that it would improve his quality of life. That weekend, his appetite was still good, and our daughter stopped by with a plain McDonald's cheeseburger, which was his favorite. Any time we would take a road trip, we would spoil him with one. At this point, we knew the ramifications would be a horrific mess, but it didn't matter. He scarfed it down like labs are known to do with food, and as long as he was eating, we still had hope.

Monday morning was a standard day at work, and I got off a little early to make it to his appointment. I remember him being excited to take a car ride, so I hobbled with him to the truck and picked him up to put him in the back seat. Odie and I took the 15-minute drive to the clinic, and the staff was helpful. We pulled up to the front door under the awning, and a staff member came out and administered the shot while he was lying in the back seat. Labradors are a breed noted for having a high pain tolerance, and Moose didn't even flinch. On the ride home, he was alert and sitting up, happy to be with Mom and Dad on an outing. The next day, he seemed to be doing better with getting up and walking, but the hope was short-lived. He was at the front window when I came home from work on Tuesday and greeted me at the door. I remember touching his ears and saying, "Hey buddy!" in the high-pitched tone he recognized as my voice of praise. I also remember missing how he used to wag his tail in anticipation of our daily greeting, a joy we had not experienced for months. The night was uneventful, but the next day, he took a turn for the worse.

Wednesday morning, Moose was barely eating enough to take his pills, but he was still eating. He wasn't, however, able to get up on his own. There were always times when he would slip on the tile floor or get stuck under a table and require help, but this was different. It was at this point that we started considering the inevitable horror of putting him down. By Thanksgiving Day, his appetite was all but gone. We had plans to go to our youngest daughter, Chelsey's apartment that night for Thanksgiving dinner since we had planned Saturday for the larger event at our house with extended family and friends. The evening was wonderful since it was just us, our three kids, and the four grandbabies. Chelsey and John have a pit mix named Luna, who was eating up the attention, and, for a short time, I experienced the joy of doting on a healthy dog with a tail wagging furiously. Deep in my soul, I had the nagging twinge of what was to come, but we had not agreed on a time. When we got home that night, he had defecated and urinated on the blanket in his special spot in the living room. He couldn't even raise his head to greet us. I tried to get him to his feet, but his body was limp and warm from lying in his urine. We cleaned him up as best we could, and I carried him to the bed.

The next morning on Friday, we encountered the same mess, but I carried him to the bathroom and laid him in the tub with his head facing away from the faucet as I gently lathered the soup on his dying body. I stroked him gently to wash away the dirt, grime, and urine. He feebly attempted to lap up the water, so I filled a cup and washed away the nasty water from his gentle face as he drank the water mixed with tears falling from my cheeks. I dried him off and, laid him back on a clean blanket and tried to get him to take his medication, but he would not eat. My wife and I both knew it was time, and I told her I would make an appointment on Monday. In retrospect, we probably should have taken him in that day, but the family was coming to the house the next day, and we wanted them to have an opportunity to say goodbye.

Saturday morning, I called the clinic and asked for an appointment at one o'clock on Monday. The receptionist asked what the appointment was for. After a short pause and with a soft voice, I said, "This will be Moose's last appointment." I don't know why I couldn't say the words, "We'll be putting him to sleep." Maybe it was because I was already going through the stages of grief and had been for some time. I was experiencing denial, but it would soon be replaced by a slew of other emotions. At three o'clock that afternoon, I texted Dr. Smith and asked if he could come in on Sunday for the procedure, fearing

Moose wouldn't make it to Monday and even if he did, he would be suffering. As always, Dr. Smith was accommodating and kind. He told me to update him on Sunday morning.

As we prepared the Thanksgiving dinner on Saturday, I was hoping the smells would spark some responsiveness, but nothing. He just lay on his blanket, breathing heavily. It was an awkward evening when the guests arrived. "Don't mind the dying dog on the living room floor." Thankfully, everyone was very understanding and offered heartfelt condolences for our precious Moose. My good buddy from childhood, Darren, came over, and we talked and laughed for hours at the bar in the kitchen. Normally, I'm a social butterfly at these functions, but I needed Darren that night and stayed with him for most of it. Darren had this to say about Moose when I asked him if he'd like to contribute to telling Moose's story.

> "I'll never forget the first time I met Moose. Jake and Odie hadn't been in OKC very long, so it was one of my first two visits to their house. Upon approaching the front door and ringing the doorbell there was a sudden smash against the front window, the blinds damn near go flying and there was this snarling/barking Chocolate Moose. It startled me and had me questioning my decision to visit. Once inside, however, there was nothing more than an extremely happy and excited puppy who was only following

natural instincts to protect his territory.

I didn't get to see Moose during his world travels once Jake and family began their trek to multiple countries but, I'm certain that he was the best travel companion. Towards the end during my visits to the house, he was aged, and his head tilted to the side, but his attitude never changed. He was the same happy puppy that I first met in 2009. The only time I ever saw him still and not feeling well was the last time I saw him. As part of the "family" I was invited over to sip bourbon and have dinner with Jake and the entire family. We ate, drank, and all dreaded the last goodbye. I leaned down several times that evening petting him, whispering in his ear that it was going to be okay and that he was Jake's best friend. He didn't move, and that's the only time I had ever seen him still. He lived a long life and brought so much joy to the entire Ivie/Saucedo family. Now, he's chasing all the toys he wants completely healthy and still happy. Cheers for Moose!"

Our son Kyle doesn't show emotions but seemed to stay in the same spot close to Moose. Our daughter Chelsey seemed to take it the hardest. She sat on the floor sobbing next to him, whispering in his ear how much she loved him. She later noted that she noticed a tear fall from his eye as she was saying goodbye.

Chelsey insisted on contributing to the book and this is what she had to say:

I remember the day we brought you home. We drove out of state just to pick you up. There was a little bed in the middle seat where you sat the whole ride home. When we finally got home you met your big sister, Ginger. You went straight to annoying her with your puppy ways, but you kept that grumpy old lady, young. I was so excited to show you to everyone. I even took you around my middle school to show my friends and teachers. I had a well thought out feeding and walking schedule that I wrote down in a notebook. I followed it for less than a week. But you still got plenty cuddles from me; you just depended upon Mom and Dad to feed you.

You have always been a gentle giant, from being goofy and clumsy when running around, and occasionally running right into a wall to being sweet and patient when young me wanted to give you a much-needed pedicure. I soaked your paws in warm water and everything. Although, Dad wasn't too fond of the pink Claire's nail polish I put on you.

Fast forward and we are moving to Europe after I graduated. Our house in Germany overlooked a huge cornfield. There was a small pathway that we would walk with you and Ginger. You got to be off leash because you are a good boy who would always come back when called. You would run free through the tall grass as fast as you could. But your pal Ginger, she was slowing down. We soon found out that she too was sick. We got her all the treatment that was available... but we eventually had to say goodbye. So then there was you - missing your sister but still as spunky as ever.

Then we moved to Italy. We were still heartbroken over Ginger, but I had been asking for a new puppy since my bed felt so empty without her. I was told no of course. But then one night under the pretense of getting pizza, we ended up getting a new puppy, Mariposa. She was crazy from the beginning, but she was meant for our family. Boy did she keep you young like you did for Ginger. You had never had a puppy around before and she was putting you through the works. But you ended up being her only friend - the only friend she will ever have.

Recently when you moved home after being away for 7 years, we both get to enjoy the house we grew up in. When I drop off Eva in the morning you sit outside my old bedroom door waiting for us. At first, I thought it was Mari because you were jumping on the door and scratching to get in, but no. For the past couple of weeks, I open the door and there you are laying right in front of it. You get up and start wagging your tail as I go to get you a treat. It is crazy to think I got you when you were just a puppy, and I was just a kid. But now you wait for my baby to drop food from her highchair, and we both have a couple grey hairs. You more than me of course. You are 91 in people years after all.

Chelsey was hurting but agreed she would join us for Moose's final moments. After everyone had their fill of delicious food and drink, they slowly started trickling out the door to go home. The silence was deafening. I picked Moose up one last time and carried him to bed. I positioned his body between my wife and me as Mariposa curled up at the foot of our king-sized bed. She had been sniffing him and was picking up on our sorrow. I was in and out of sleep the entire night, keeping my hand on his neck, massaging the scruff, and dreading the task at hand.

The morning of 26 Nov 2023 was my 27th anniversary of enlisting in the Air Force as an eighteen-year-old kid, but it was only in retrospect that I considered the significance. Moose was still breathing, but his condition had not improved. I transferred his warm body to his special spot with a clean blanket and let him rest undisturbed. We told Chelsey that the appointment was set for noon, and she came to the house to go with us. I retrieved our cat, Isabella, from her room to say goodbye to her brother, but she simply jumped out of my arms and ran away. It's difficult to understand the minds of our furry companions, but I didn't press the issue. The weather that morning was cold, and it seemed like the Oklahoma wind was particularly inhospitable. We didn't bother taking him outside to do his business, but Mariposa had no issues racing out the back door to torment the neighbor's dog. We had agreed that Mariposa should be there for closure and began getting her harness and muzzle together. Moose's harness hung lifelessly on the doggy tail hanger in the laundry room, never to be used again. The feeling in the house was hard to explain. It was mournful but, at the same time, deliberate. Although the task at hand was a hard one, everyone seemed unified in the effort to complete it.

I pulled the Tahoe out of the garage and closed the garage door. I opened the hatch and returned inside to retrieve my lifelong buddy for his final ride as my living companion for over fourteen years. I knelt next to Moose and softly worked my left arm under his shoulder and my right arm under his hips. His muscles were unresponsive except for the sighs of pain as I picked him up and carried him out. I gently placed him in the back of the Tahoe with his head facing the front. I had configured two straps to connect to the ring on their matching harnesses at the chest, which were of just the right length to prevent Moose and Mariposa from getting tangled on long road trips. There was no threat of tangling on this trip as I returned to the house for Mariposa and situated her next to her brother. I attached her harness to her respective side to prevent her from "losing her coco puffs" and trampling poor Moose. Odie inspected the setup and petted his head before she opened the passenger door and sat in the front seat. Chelsey entered the car and took a seat in the back behind me as we backed out of the driveway and proceeded to the clinic.

The ride to the clinic was quietly somber. We left thirty minutes before noon and avoided the church crowd, although it was not by design since hymns and spirituality were starting to take shape outside the realm of organized religion. We were on one last ride with Moose and would soon say goodbye. I don't remember anything noteworthy along the ride there; my eyes were clouded from a lack of sleep and dry from crying the night before. It was as if the whole world had ceased to exist outside of a bubble surrounding the five souls in a crudely manufactured man-made machine as one of God's perfect creations crumbled in the cargo space behind us. I drove slower than I normally do, as if the difference of five miles per hour would somehow make it better. Or perhaps I simply wasn't focused on the normal rush of everyday life since I was relearning the precious value unique to time and precious moments. Sometimes, we don't even realize the most significant moments of our lives until after those moments have passed. I was not about to have that happen...so I drove slowly and deliberately.

We arrived at the clinic about ten minutes early despite my deliberate pace. We pulled up to the same awning where Moose had received his shot a week earlier. Dr. Smith met us outside, and I was lost because I didn't know which steps to take next. As mentioned earlier, Odie and Chelsey carried the weight of releasing Ginger of her pain while I was deployed to the Middle East, so this would be my first time experiencing the sorrow firsthand. I have heard of people who are either unwilling or unable to be there when their fur baby transitions to the other side. Wrong, right, or indifferent, my personal opinion is that a puppy parent owes it to their loyal companion to stay until the final moment. Call me judgmental if you will, but I consider it cowardice to have someone else bear that burden and abandon a dog who has done nothing but devote his entire existence in loyalty for the happiness of his owner alone to leave the physical world. As for when the decision should be made, it is entirely up to the animal's caretaker. In the case of Moose, he communicated it was time, and he was ready. I remember on those nights when he would have a bad day, whispering in his ear that he needed to let us know when it was time, which he did. It wasn't easier, but it was clear, and clarity is what Odie and I needed.

I parked the car and opened the hatch to let Mari out and put on her muzzle. She barked a little at the vet, but we were able to calm her down. Chelsey took her leash as I picked up Moose from the back and followed Dr. Smith into the building. He warned me about some ice that had frozen from rain the night before as I carried my little buddy into the facility. I must hand it to the staff who had set up the room beautifully. There were chairs around the outside and a rug to lay him down in the center of the floor. Dr Smith told us to take a few minutes, and he would return to "borrow" Moose for his IV. He mentioned that with old dogs in this condition, it was often hard to find the vein. Then he softly closed the door. On a nearby veranda was an example of the cremation package showing options. For a fleeting moment, I thought of all the families who had been in this room about to go through what we had yet to experience. The moment soon passed, and the sorrow returned. I hesitate to use the word selfish, but in a way, that's how I felt. I didn't care about anyone else's situation or how they had to put their fur baby down. I was only concerned about what my family was feeling. Dr Smith returned and gently picked up our precious Moose. He mentioned something as he carried Moose out for his IV, but I didn't hear what he said.

After he left the room, we were left to talk about the options and agreed on the cremation package, which had a plaster casting of a paw and a nicely crafted cedar box for the ashes. Surprisingly, I was able to keep my composure at first. It was as if there was a task at hand to distract me from my emotions. The memories began to flood my mind so thickly that I felt I had to brush them away from my face. Dr. Smith returned alone after a while, at which time we told him which package we'd like to purchase.

He agreed that it was a nice package and mentioned he had thirteen of them on his mantle at home. He explained that the procedure would involve two injections, the first of which was a sedative and the second which would release Moose. He once again left and returned with a small slip of paper on which the cost was written. Come to find out, the words he said that I didn't catch were that he would return with a price. I won't mention the cost, but it wasn't astronomic and paled in comparison to the cost of his health insurance, medicine, and treatment up to this point. Odie and I agreed a long time ago that price points were irrelevant if it bought us time.

Dr Smith's next entry to the room was with Moose draped in a soft blanket. He positioned our precious baby on his belly with his head between his front paws. We gently stroked his head as he lay on the floor, and Dr. Smith administered the first injection. We could feel his body loosen up as his breathing steadied, and he began to relax. The sedative made him a little sick, and Dr. Smith cleaned up the small amount of fluid seeping from his mouth. I pulled Mariposa over to him and told her to say goodbye to her brother. She sniffed him and then turned back to me with a confused look in her eye. She quietly sat next to me, watching the entire time as if she knew and understood but didn't fully comprehend. This next part gets a little rough, so read on at your own risk, and I'll attempt to capture the feelings experienced by my family.

Dr. Smith told us it was time and recommended we sit down and pet him while talking to him. This was when I really started to lose it. I choked back the tears as I rubbed his ears and massaged his head. I'd like to believe he could hear us speaking nothing but comforting words and that he could feel the love. We all were crying, and my wife reached over and touched my arm. She was attempting to comfort me, but it wasn't working. Don't get me wrong, the gesture was sweet, but I was inconsolable at this point. We continued talking to him, telling him we loved him and that he was the best boy ever. I saw out of the corner of my eye that Dr. Smith had pulled out the second injection and glanced over as he squeezed the syringe until nothing was left. I wept like I had never wept before as the chemicals took over, and I felt the life leave his ailing body with one last breath. I cried aloud, "He's gone, babe...he's gone!" as I turned my head away. It seemed like an eternity before I could muster up the courage to turn back toward the shell that was once my dog, my best friend, my companion. When I did, I saw Dr Smith pull out his stethoscope and check for a heartbeat. I'll never forget the finality of his words when he said, "He's passed." I finally caught my breath from sobbing and touched him one last time as Mariposa sniffed him. We all got up and were crying as we left the room. All of us glanced back one last time to see his chocolate brown fur, his soft ears, and his raspberry nose as we left the room.

On the way out, Dr. Smith assured us that the company they used for the cremation was legitimate and that they would take good care of Moose and treat his body with respect. He said that they had a method of tracking the body and ensuring the ashes would be his and not mixed with any other ashes. He told us to expect a call in about a week to come pick them up. We thanked him and gave him a hug as we exited the building and got in the car with Mariposa for an emotional ride home. I was slow and deliberate, just like an hour before, but this was a different feeling. This time, there was no mission, no task at hand to dread. It was over, and this ride was the beginning of a long journey toward recovery and embracing the grieving process.

## CHAPTER 8:

## LEARNING TO MOVE ON

That afternoon was hard to describe. I'm not proud of it by any means, but I went straight to the whiskey, and Odie went straight to nap time. We were both exhausted, but I got right back into what felt comfortable for me, and that was a glass of whiskey in the spare room in my comfy chair in front of a small TV. When Moose could still climb stairs, my go-to spot for watching movies or playing video games was upstairs, where the widescreen TV and the lazy boy recliner were located. However, after he fell ill, I relocated my video game consoles to the spare room. It worked out great for a few reasons. When Karmine would stay with us, he could go to bed in the same room, and I could unwind. Another benefit was that Moose had easy access to me and I to him. I would often be sitting in my wooden wagon-wheel chair handed down to me by my grandfather, and I would hear Moose come wandering in. I would always pause whatever I was doing, rub his ears, and ask how he was doing. Mariposa, the attention hound, would always break in and steal my attention, but a little bit of love always went a long way with Moose. Sometimes, he would lie down in the room, but most times, he would wander back out and lie down in his special spot in the living room.

On this particular afternoon, I wasn't in the mood to play games, so I watched TV. I had been on a western kick, so I was watching either an HBO miniseries or a movie. Maybe I watched both. It's hard to remember the specifics, but I remember numerous bouts of tears. I would get into the plot of the bad guy committing atrocities against the good town folk. The hero would step in, and then it would hit me again like a freight train that he was gone. He would never again come to check on me while I played my games or watched TV. I would never again sigh because I had just got comfortable, and I had to get up to let him outside. No, those moments were forever a thing of the past, and now I would give anything to be "inconvenienced" again by his needs. So, I sat there drinking whiskey and wallowing in self-pity.

Occasionally, I would think of a moment or a memory and feel a sense of warmth, knowing that the only reason I was hurting so bad was because I had loved him so much. As I got up to fill my glass of whiskey after an episode had concluded, I thought about playing my favorite game, Fallout. I was currently working on a second playthrough of New Vegas and remembered how fun Fallout 4 was since you could build your own settlements and recruit people and pets. I hadn't played Fallout 4 in months, but it suddenly hit me that I had purchased an add-on that allowed pets in addition to the standard German Shepherd named "Dogmeat." So, being the nerd that I am, I remembered that I had created a chocolate lab character and named him something from a preselected list of options. Months ago, I went through the build menu and created two dog houses with accompanying dog bowls and neon signs that said Moose and Mariposa. The cool thing about this setup is if I would wait long enough, both characters would get in their dog houses and sit with their heads poking out. It was a fun feature in the game that I hadn't played in forever, but it served as an example of memory triggers that would constantly remind me of the gaping chasm in my heart.

I was in a very dark place that afternoon and evening. I won't say that I was suicidal because I still have so much to live for with my kids and grandkids, but I will say there were fleeting moments. These moments were coupled with a feeling of despair and the want to not be here, away from my Moose. The thoughts would whisper to me, "You should be with him" or "Why bother? Your life will never be the same." I'm sure the alcohol didn't help, but it made me realize that emotional trauma is real and the triggers casting people into a fit of depression vary as much as personalities in people and animals alike. Before Moose taught me how to love, I was highly unempathetic towards people. I had a "get tough or die" mentality when people would talk about their problems or seek comfort. But now I was getting a taste of my own medicine and experiencing first-hand what depression is.

As I mentioned before, it was Sunday at 1200 when we took Moose in for his final appointment, and I was able to drink whiskey all afternoon because I had a boss who was empathetic. I had told JC before that I had an appointment for Monday, and he said just take the day off. He had shared with me his experience with his dog a few years earlier, so he got it and told me to take Monday off, even knowing the plan had changed, and we had put Moose down on Sunday. I needed that day. I spent the day finding old pictures of Moose and texting close friends. I posted the obligatory social media content on his passing, and the notes of condolences came flooding in. My close friend, Brad, probably empathized with me the most since he had lost Nike and Mia a few years earlier. His generosity came shining through when I received a text that he had coordinated a bottle of whiskey to be sent to the house. The delivery guy came around 1500 and read the note. Then he said he was personally very sorry for our loss. I gave the poor guy an awkward hug and told him, "Thank you." The whiskey Brad bought me was called Angel's Envy.

I went to bed on Sunday night, and despite the many glasses of whiskey, I could not sleep. I lay there with my eyes closed and would see my buddy's face in the darkness as if he was floating through an abyss like the wind. He would appear and then disappear like an apparition in a scary movie. It was the strangest thing, but it kept me awake for what seemed like hours. I finally fell asleep and rose the next morning to the sound of Chelsey bringing Evalyn over for Nana's Day Care.

I don't remember being particularly hungover, but I had little interest in normal hygiene routines. I felt numb and had zero interest in doing things. It was good that I didn't go to work that day because I was in no mood to deal with what seemed to me to be petty and insignificant problems. I waited until noon after Chelsey picked up Evalyn to start drinking whiskey again, but this time, it wasn't to numb the pain since I was already numb. I don't remember shedding a single tear on Monday.

I sat in my room with Mariposa, whom I hadn't mentioned yet, and was in a severe state of depression as well. I just talked to her and said soothing things like, "I know you miss him" or "Dad loves you." She seemed especially attentive and responsive to my love, and it provided some comfort knowing I wasn't alone and we still had Mariposa to care for. I got up and let her outside as she slowly exited the house, which was unlike her. She was sniffing the ground, and for the first time in months, I actually paid attention to her as she wandered around doing her business. Before, I was holding Moose or following him to make sure he didn't fall and never paid attention to Mariposa's habits. A previous commander and close friend, Jason Zemler, once told me after I had disappointing news, "Ivan, (that's my callsign) take a day and be mad. That's your right. But move past it." It was at this moment that I decided I had to move on.

I went back inside and started jotting things down on my phone that I remembered about Moose. As I typed, I could feel myself smile. Then, I would look up in thought and jot something else down. The memories came pouring in, and I couldn't type fast enough on my phone. Whatever was on the TV was being ignored because I was one glass of whiskey in, and the creative juices were flowing. I thought to myself, "This goofy and adorable dog has experienced in fourteen years more than most people experience in a lifetime!" And that's when the crazy idea hit me. "I'm going to write a book!" Then, the self-doubt kicked in, but I suppressed it and continued with an outline. I began to take some sage advice from my father, who once asked me, "Son, how do you eat an elephant?" I was young and struggling with my first year in the Air Force and a very challenging language course in Russian. I replied, "I don't know, dad." "One bite at a time, son." So, I harnessed that hunger and started chomping away at this elephant that you are now reading.

When Odie awoke from her nap and started tooling around the kitchen, I was hesitant to tell her of my plan. It has zero to do with her support for me, which has always been at a level I don't deserve. It was more because I had my doubts. First, I had doubts as to whether I could write something other people would want to read. Second, I doubted if I had enough material. Third, I doubted whether I could complete the publishing process. But I took all those doubts and brushed them aside. I walked into the kitchen and said, "Babe, let me ask you something." I paused. "What would you say if I were to write a book about Moose?" I expected her pragmatic and practical mindset to take over, but she was unconditionally supportive. I think she knows me well enough that whether I was actually going to write a book or not,

I needed to hear that it was a good idea (words of affirmation and all that). So, the journey began.

I mentioned depression earlier, but I'd like to talk through what I experienced in the weeks following Moose's passing. It was a flurry of emotions and a very rough time for me. I'd like to use the backdrop of the five stages of grief to bin these feelings into compartments, but I feel some will inevitably blend into others. According to experts, the five stages of grief are denial, anger, depression, bargaining, and acceptance. I did not experience these phases in a linear and chronological order. They were mixed, combined, randomized, and sometimes sudden. Additionally, not all of them manifested only after his passing. The grieving process for me began when he got sick for the first time in the summer of 2022 and continues even now. Denial was one that manifested before he passed.

The first instance of denial I experienced would have to be right when Moose got sick in the summer of 2022. It was so sudden, and I just couldn't believe that he had cancer. Two days before, he was jumping around the backyard. Although they never officially diagnosed him with cancer, I could tell he was starting to lose mobility due to the osteoarthritis. We put him on Gabapentin, and he was still able to jump on and off the sofa. So, in a sense, I beat the first bout of denial because we were able to nurse him back to health for a few months before he came down with vestibular disease. The second example of denial would be that week before he passed when I recommended to Odie that we try the shot. I most certainly was in denial about his condition. I would soon realize that it doesn't matter how much you tell yourself it isn't going to happen. The inevitable day will always come. Death seeks us all out eventually.

I would say the bargaining piece ties in closely with the denial aspect of the grieving process. Odie and I felt that if we bought him the right supplements and the right medicine, he would be okay. As mentioned before, it did work for a short time. Now, if you're thinking, I prayed to God that if He would let Moose live, I would quit drinking or eradicate some other vice from life, that wasn't the case at all. I was very pleased that fate allowed us to spend the time we had with him. I suppose on a subconscious level, I would think to myself, "Please don't let today be the day!" We were always hoping he would make it to the next event, whether that be Halloween, a trip to the lake, or just the upcoming weekend. Eventually, though, time ran out, and we were left with only the memories of how we used that time.

Now, let's talk anger. This one was a weird one to pin down because the anger didn't manifest in a manner that was directly associated with Moose's death. I wasn't angry at God; I wasn't angry at the vet or my wife, and I surely wasn't angry with Moose. It wasn't like he had committed suicide or done something that got him hurt. He hung on to the very end and always had the sweetest demeanor. You hear of dogs that get cantankerous in their old age or lose their hearing and get startled, resulting in a person getting bitten. This wasn't Moose at all. He was mostly happy even though his normal everyday life was full of pain. No, the anger piece was more insidious in its manifestation.

Anger became a thing on Wednesday morning when I left for work. It was a normal morning of hopping in the shower and putting on my flight suit. I ate breakfast and visited with Chelsey and Evalyn. I left the house melancholy but ready to face the day. As I was turning left out of the housing area at a particularly dangerous intersection, I was behind a person who, in my mind, was being *way* too cautious. Opportunity after opportunity came and went without this person moving. I was beginning to see red. I tend to be impatient with other drivers, but I wanted to push this person into oncoming traffic. I was so enraged. When she finally pulled out, I floored it right behind her, squealing the tires and passing her on the right. As I glared at her, I saw she had kids in the car, and I felt like a giant tool. As I continued driving, I got into a short conversation in my own head about the meaning of this exchange with a stranger. A voice in my head told me, "Things like this build character." I audibly spoke these words in the cab of my truck: "I don't want strong character! I want my fucking dog back!" Then I broke down right there in the truck. I won't deny that I was a giant jerk that morning, but it taught me that once I figured out what was eating at me, I was able to move on with the rest of my day without being a jerk to another person. It also taught me that you never know what battles people are facing in their lives that may make them act out of character. One thing I know for a fact is that that morning, I did not want any divine lessons about patience, but I probably needed them.

I touched on the depression the day of Moose's passing and the day after, but the next few weeks were definitely gloomy. Now I know why the Air Force asks us questions at our annual physicals about how many times over the last few months we have had little interest in doing things. That was how I felt. Our calendar was chocked full of birthdays, Christmas events, sports practices, and random stuff to do. I didn't want to do any of it. I went through the motions of going to work but my heart wasn't in it. My subordinates would come to me with complaints about inefficient processes and ingenious ways of solving problems. I just didn't care. Oh, I faked interest and told them how much of a good job they were doing, but I quite frankly didn't' give two poops. That first week I didn't want to do much of anything. We didn't even put up the Christmas tree or lights. Odie referred to the Christmas of 2023 as the Black Christmas...and it was. That week would close out with one last task.

On Friday, I received a phone call that Moose's ashes were ready to be picked up. I would not be able to make it in time to pick them up on Friday, so I told the receptionist that I would pick them up on Monday since we also had Karmine's basketball game on Saturday morning. This decision did not sit well with me for some reason, so I told Odie I would forego sleeping in and get up early enough to get Moose and make it back for the game. I left around 0730 in the morning and arrived right as they were opening. I softly said, "I'm here to pick up Moose." The young lady went into a room and brought out a bag with his name on it. I waited to open the bag until I got home so Odie and I could do it together. I put the bag in the passenger seat of my truck as Moose and I set out on one final ride. I could almost see him there panting and smiling as I drove down the street I had driven so many times before. I pulled into the driveway teary-eyed after completing this last final step to bring Moose home. It was at this point that I began to feel the comforting feeling of acceptance. All the tasks had been done, from adopting Moose and raising him, transporting his fuzzy butt across the globe on countless adventures, caring for him when his health deteriorated, and being there in that final moment when he took his last breath and was released from his pain. Now, he sits on our mantle next to Ginger in a small cedar box that simply reads, "Moose 30/03/09 – 26/11/23".

I was going to conclude this chapter and the book with the previous paragraph, but in the weeks after finishing it and leading up to New Year's Day, I noticed that Mariposa, like me, was not quite herself. We took a road trip to see Odie's sister in Independence, Missouri, for our great-nephew's birthday. We loaded up Mariposa in the Tahoe, and I was able to lengthen her tether since I didn't have to worry about her getting tangled with Moose. The events of the weekend were enjoyable since we saw family, but the return trip was when Mari started to show other symptoms. She stopped eating and had diarrhea. This went on for a few days, and Odie and I were worried. On the day when I decided I was going to take her to the vet, she pulled a Moose and snapped right out of it. I can only speculate why she was feeling poorly, but it was most likely the stress of the trip coupled with returning home to a house where she probably expected Moose to be.

The next few weeks, she would sniff his spot and lay on the bed with me in the guest bedroom with her head facing where he would lay on the floor. On the nights when we had the grandkids, I would sleep in the spare room with Karmine. Mari would sleep on the bed while we would put Moose on his blanket at the foot of the bed. She would always warn me when Moose needed to go out, albeit sometimes too late. But when she and I would hang out in there, she seemed less alert and wouldn't even stir when I would make a noise by shifting in my chair or opening a beer. She's doing better now, but I can tell she misses him.

The week of Christmas was strange. Everyone else seemed festive and cheery, but it was hard to get into the Christmas spirit. This week, I experienced another emotion, fear. I found myself not being as sad and enjoying writing about Moose. One night, as I was trying to go to sleep, I found myself filled with dread. I was afraid that the sense of normalcy would return but be accompanied by forgetting him. I dreaded the thought of grieving him, but at the same time, I wanted to embrace it because I feared it would lead to him being forgotten. I grabbed my phone and started jotting down more memories about which you are reading in these last few chapters. That gave me hope, and I realized that starting to feel normal was not a betrayal of his memory. I look toward 2024 with this hope and sincerely hope that the words captured in this work will touch the readers in a positive way, just as Moose touched the lives of so many.

Toward the end of January, I was getting back into the swing of work after the "holiday hangover" where people tend to be less motivated from the cold of winter and the daunting idea of returning to the grind. One night I went to bed early because I had an early show the next morning for a certification flight where I would be evaluated on my ability to lead a crew through a mission. I thought as I laid in bed how nice it would be to dream of my little buddy. The dreams came with a vengeance.

The night was plagued between being in and out of sleep. It's always hard to sleep when you know you have to awake at three A.M. I would drift off and begin dreaming only to be startled awake. The dreams were mostly unremarkable until I drifted off about midnight. I remember I was in a familiar place. I was at my grandparents' property that I had purchased as our retirement getaway. I was with Moose, and we were about to retire for the evening. I ushered him into the house and was about to follow when I was suddenly attacked by a bobcat. I awoke to Odie touching me asking why I was screaming in my sleep.

I've always felt that dreams are a surreal reflection of our subliminal thoughts. I initially thought the bobcat represented the stress I was feeling regarding my mission which would begin a few hours later. I dismissed it as such and proceeded to do well on the mission at hand. In retrospect after talking to Odie who told me she felt no anxiety from me regarding my mission the next day, I realized that the bobcat was not a representation of my job stress. Rather, it was the representation of how grief will pounce on you at an unsuspected time. The bobcat attacking me unannounced was my subliminal interpretation of how after I led Moose into a safe space in death, I was still vulnerable and would be for some time.

Mourning is a journey that doesn't end after loss. I sincerely hope that the words captured in this work have touched you, the reader, in a positive way just as Moose touched the lives of so many. I'll close this book with a modified quote from the miniseries 1883, "Moose out-smiled me, outloved me, outfought me, outlived me, he's outlived all of us." I miss you, buddy.

*The last big adventure at the lake with Mariposa and Odie*

# ABOUT THE AUTHOR

*Jake "Ivan" Ivie is a Lieutenant Colonel combat aviator with 27 years of active duty time in the US Air Force. He currently serves as the Director of Operations for the 963rd Airborne Air Control Squadron at Tinker Air Force Base in Oklahoma City. He is married to his wife of 20 years, retired Air Force Technical Sergeant, Odie Ivie and has three grown step-children – Brittany (33), Kyle (30), Chelsey (26) and four grandchildren – Karmine (10), Enilia (5), Evalyn (2) and Esker (2). He has flown on varying platforms in the Air Force with six deployments in support of Operations ALLIED FORCE, NORTHERN WATCH, IRAQI FREEDOM, ENDURING FREEDOM, INHERENT RESOLVE, and RESOLUTE SUPPORT. Permanent duty stations include Spangdahlem Air Base in Germany, Aviano Air Base in Italy, Kadena Air Base in Okinawa, and several locations in the United States. Hobbies include fishing, woodworking, blade smithing, video games and of course spending time with his grandchildren.*

www.ingramcontent.com/pod-product-compliance
Lightning Source LLC
Chambersburg PA
CBHW060529130626
46553CB00002B/693